A gift for

_____

the lovely bride

from

_____

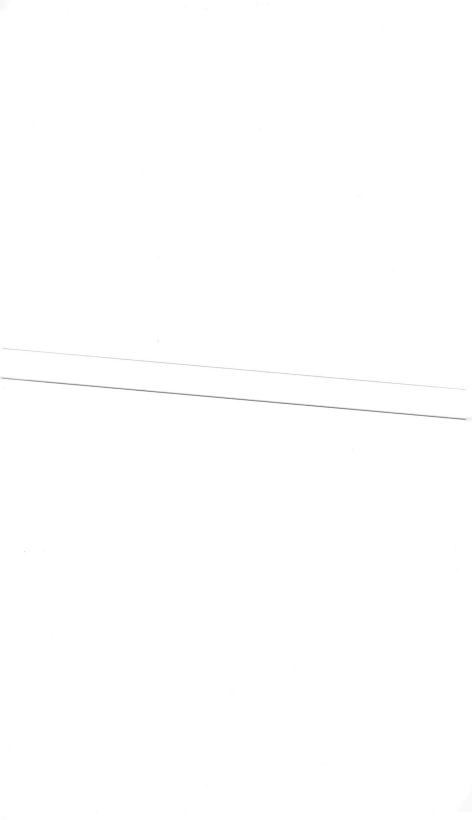

A Bride's First Cookbook

I Do...
Not Cook

Tips, recipes and advice for the newlywed cook

I Do...Not Cook is a collection of easy yet elegant dishes for the new bride or the beginning cook. Recipes and information on the following pages were designed with the novice chef in mind. Even those who have never created a solo dinner should have no trouble making masterpiece meals using this book's simple directions.

Some of these recipes are hand-me-down favorites. Others add a new twist to old standards. With *I Do...Not Cook* you're sure to find plenty of ideas for feeding your spouse and keeping your home running in top form.

Publisher: Scott Morris
Editors: Tara Harris and Jen Osborn
Recipe Editor: Cheryl Morris
Recipe Compilation: Norma Guge
Cover Design: Erin Smith
Interior Design: Michelle Meyer

ISBN 1-57502-751-8

Published and Printed by:
Morris Press Cookbooks
3212 East Highway 30
Kearney, NE 68847
www.morriscookbooks.com
800-445-6621

Table of Contents

Introduction vii

Breakfast in Bed 1

Before Things
    Get Cooking 11

Lovin' From
    The Oven 25

Hot, Hot, Hot! 35

Getting Fresh 43

Extra Flavors,
    Extra Fun 53

Main Squeeze 69

Sweet Stuff 93

Index

Recipe For A Happy Marriage

3 c. love
1 c. consideration
2 c. flattery, carefully concealed
2 c. human kindness
1 pkg. hard work
1 gal. faith in each other
2 c. praise
1 reasonable budget
1 c. courtesy
1 pkg. playfulness

1 sm. pinch of in-laws
1 generous dash of cooperation
2 tsp. pure extract of "I Am Sorry"
1 c. contentment
1 portion patience
1 c. confidence
1 lg. portion understanding
1 c. encouragement
1 lg. or several sm. hobbies
5 c. kisses and pecks

Flavor with frequent portions of recreation and a dash of happy memories. Stir well and remove any specks of jealousy, temper or criticism. Sweeten well with generous portions of love and keep warm with a steady flame of devotion. Never serve with a cold shoulder or a hot tongue.

How To Bring Some Lovin'
To Your Oven

Grandmother always said "The way to a man's heart is through his stomach." While this isn't always true, almost every wife wants to entice her husband with the comfort foods he loved as a child. This can be a daunting task for a beginning cook. If the idea of preparing a meal from top to bottom leaves you in a cold sweat, take a deep breath and relax. You're not alone. For most women, excellence in the kitchen is a work in progress. Start with what you know and go from there. Keep working at it and you'll be queen of the kitchen before you know it.

The Cooking Cycle

In the past, women handed down their kitchen expertise to their daughters, who generally went straight from their parent's house to their husband's home. These dutiful little girls spent their formative years at their mother's apron strings, waiting anxiously for every cooking lesson. It was a mother's obligation to prepare her daughters for the responsibility of cooking for a family, and most daughters happily complied.

An old Italian practice took the daily cooking lessons a step further. According to tradition, women in the community compiled their favorite recipes, bound them in a hand-crafted cookbook and presented the treasured dishes to the bride as part of her dowry. Those brides, the ones who grew up in the kitchen, probably didn't have much trouble making the transition from their mother's stove to their own.

Even if today's kitchen training isn't as formalized as it used to be, you probably still grew up watching Mom prepare many creative suppers. It's hard to imagine she was ever a bumbling cook in her own kitchen. Chances are your mother faced the same fears as a novice chef that you face today. Step by step, little by little, she mastered the art of feeding her family mouth-watering meals. After a little practice, you will too.

The Liberated Cook

Today's kitchen is a whole new frontier. In recent decades women have challenged historical roles, taken briefcase in hand and entered the workplace. In addition to altering the face of the corporate world, daughters of the baby-boom generation are still in charge of putting a meal on the table. But now they don't always have the knowledge handed down by their mothers and grandmothers, or the time to slave over a four-course meal.

This common predicament fills many of us with romantic notions of making enough money to hire a live-in cook who would be ready at our beck and call. In moments of pure delusion we might even imagine the love of our life having a hot meal waiting for us when we walk through the door after a hard day at the office. Putting aside birthdays and make-up meals after a big fight, the truth is that you're probably going to be the one doing most of the cooking.

Sharing the Kitchen

Still, a new bride shouldn't let kitchen duties be the iron yoke of her marriage. The kitchen can be a place of communion instead of an isolation cell. While most brides have to bribe their hubby into cooking breakfast in bed for them, some are lucky enough to have a man who knows his way around the kitchen — or is at least ready and willing to learn.

If you believe the expression "Too many cooks will spoil the soup," you may want to change your thinking. Even if you consider yourself master of at least one room in the house, the one with all the important appliances, it can be nice to get a little help now and then. Double-teaming can save time and send you and your spouse down the aisle to culinary greatness. And, as a wise person once said, "Couples who play together stay together" — even if that playing is learning to twist new types of breads.

In fact, in these days of dual-income households, it's not uncommon for both husband and wife to man the kitchen. Some couples may even find the perfect anniversary gift is lessons at a local cooking school. Taking the classes together is another way to add precious quality time to your relationship while giving you the opportunity to sharpen your skills. And it can be fun fiddling with interesting kitchen gadgets while you and your hubby don matching aprons.

This Bride Really Cooks

Maybe you received this book as a bridal shower gift or Mom, worried about the health of her future son-in-law, wanted to give you a few hints. Whatever the reason, you'll find a variety of unique recipes created especially for people like you, a cook with minimal experience. Most of the recipes don't take much time to create and master, and rely on the basics to help get you started on the road to culinary nirvana. In general, these recipes create two to six serving portions, but can be easily adapted to satisfy a larger hungry mob. And remember, a four-serving dish is just about perfect for feeding a couple. You'll probably even have enough left over for lunch at work the next day.

If you've been cooking for years, don't automatically file this book on the shelf, just to pull out whenever the gift giver drops by. You just might discover a few tasty concoctions you've never considered before or generate a couple of ideas to put a spin on an old classic. You can even loan it to a less experienced spouse to help him find his footing in the kitchen.

Hey Honey! What's for Dinner?

Sprinkled throughout the pages of this book you'll find ingenious ideas on stocking your pantry, choosing the right tools to get started, making your own household cleaners, decorating your table, caring for your elegant dishes and utensils, creating great meals on a small budget, storing and enjoying your wedding cake and other general tips that will help make meal times as hassle-free as possible. Still, these ideas are only the beginning. Your local library and the Internet are full of other creative housekeeping options. Who's to know if you adapt suggestions from home decorating magazines? Be unique — go crazy. It's your house to run however you please.

So here's your chance. Take a deep breath, grab one of the aprons you received as a shower gift and go for it. You have all the tools and know-how it takes to get started. Just keep experimenting and before you know it you'll amaze yourself with your own culinary creations. Good luck and good cooking!

Our First Married Meal

When: _____

_____

Where: _____

_____

The Setting: _____

_____

The Menu: _____

_____

_____

_____

_____

_____

Our Special Thoughts
and Memories:

_____

_____

_____

_____

_____

_____

_____

_____

_____

_____

BREAKFAST
IN BED

Breakfast

Prepping a Perfect Pantry
A guide to buying all the essential foods you need to get started

You wouldn't drive a car without first filling it with gas and making sure the tires have enough air. Likewise, there are some essentials every bride's kitchen needs to keep it running in top form and to save the cook's helper from constant trips to the nearest convenience store.

Once you've logged in a few hours behind your stove you may be able to judge what cooking items are absolute musts and which ones are occasional foodstuffs you can beg, borrow or steal from a neighbor. Until you become master of your own culinary domain, we've listed a few favorites to ready your pantry for most recipe needs. While you're at it, don't forget all the old standbys like milk, eggs, sugar, butter and flour.

Baking chocolate
Baking powder
Baking soda
Barbecue sauce
Bouillon
Breadcrumbs
Chicken broth
Cocoa powder
Cornstarch
Evaporated milk
Flour
Gelatin, flavored or plain
Garlic
Honey
Hot sauce
Ketchup
Lemon juice
Mayonnaise or salad dressing
Mustard, dried and prepared
Nonstick cooking spray

Nuts
Olive oil
Pasta
Rice
Shortening
Soy sauce
Spices
    cinnamon, basil, garlic salt or
    powder, nutmeg, onion salt or
    dehydrated onion, oregano,
    paprika, parsley, salt and pepper
Sweetened condensed milk
Tomato paste and sauce
Tuna
Vanilla extract
Vegetable oil
Vinegars
Worcestershire sauce
Yeast

Breakfast In Bed

♥ FALLING IN LOVE FRENCH TOAST ♥

2 eggs	5 (1-inch-thick) slices French bread
½ c. milk	or Texas Toast or 6 slices dry
¼ tsp. vanilla	white bread
⅛ tsp. ground cinnamon	Margarine
	Favorite syrup or topping (opt.)

In a shallow bowl beat together eggs, milk, vanilla and cinnamon. Dip bread in mixture, coating both sides thoroughly. Use French bread for a custard-like center; Texas Toast for a thicker, heartier toast; or sliced dry white bread for a toasty, crisp French toast. In a skillet or on a griddle cook bread in a small amount of hot margarine over medium heat for 2 to 3 minutes on each side or until golden brown. Add margarine as needed. Top as desired. Yield: 2 servings.

♥ WONDERFUL WAFFLES ♥

3 eggs	1 tsp. salt
2 c. milk	2 T. butter, melted
1 c. cream	3 c. flour
⅔ tsp. baking soda, dissolved in	1½ tsp. cream of tartar
hot water	Favorite syrup or topping (opt.)

Heat waffle iron and grease according to manufacturer's instructions while mixing batter. Separate egg yolks from whites. Beat egg yolks. Add milk, cream, soda water mixture, salt, butter and flour. Beat until smooth. To egg whites add cream of tartar. Beat until stiff. Fold into batter and pour over hot waffle iron. Amount of batter used per waffle depends on size of iron. Top as desired. Yield: 4 servings.

♥ PANCAKES FOR TWO ♥

1 c. flour, sifted
¼ tsp. salt
2 tsp. baking powder
½ tsp. baking soda

1 egg, separated
1 T. oil
1 c. buttermilk
Favorite syrup or topping (opt.)

Sift flour, salt, baking powder and baking soda together. In mixing bowl beat egg yolk. Add oil and buttermilk. Add flour mixture and stir gently. Fold in beaten egg white. Let stand 8 minutes before baking on ungreased griddle or skillet. Top as desired. Yield: 2 servings.

♥ CINNAMON ROLLS FOR YOUR SWEETIE ♥

1 (12-roll) pkg. frozen dinner rolls
½ c. sugar
1 tsp. cinnamon

¾ stick butter, melted
Chopped pecans

Thaw rolls 1½ minutes on high in microwave. Mix sugar and cinnamon together. Roll dinner rolls in butter, cinnamon and sugar. Butter again; add nuts. Place in greased 9 x 9-inch pan. Let rise for 1½ to 2 hours in oven over a pan containing warm water. Bake for 20 minutes at 350°. Yield: 4 servings.

♥ APPLE OF MY EYE ROLLS ♥

½ c. brown sugar, packed
½ c. heavy whipping cream
¼ c. pecans, chopped

1 (11-oz.) can refrigerated
  breadstick dough
⅓ c. applesauce
¼ tsp. ground cinnamon

Heat oven to 350°. Mix brown sugar and cream in ungreased round 8 x 1½-inch pan. Sprinkle with pecans. Unroll breadstick dough. Do not separate. Stir together applesauce and cinnamon. Spread applesauce over dough. Roll up dough from short end. Separate at perforations. Place rolled dough in pan. Bake 15 to 20 minutes or until golden brown. Cool 1 minute. Invert pan onto serving plate. Let stand 1 minute to let caramel spread. Yield: 4 servings.

"Thou art to me a delicious torment."
--Ralph Waldo Emerson

♥ FOR MY BRAN MAN MUFFINS ♥

2 c. all-purpose flour
1½ c. bran
1½ tsp. baking soda
½ tsp. salt
1 egg

2 c. plain yogurt
½ c. oil
½ c. dark molasses or brown sugar
⅔ c. raisins

Thoroughly combine flour, bran, baking soda and salt in a large mixing bowl. Whisk together egg, yogurt, oil, molasses or brown sugar and raisins in another bowl. Make a well in the center of the dry ingredients and pour in liquid, stirring just until moist. Do not overmix. Spoon into greased muffin tins and bake at 425° for 20 to 25 minutes or until muffins are set. Yield: approximately 1 dozen muffins.

♥ MOIST COFFEE CAKE ♥

1¾ c. all-purpose flour
½ c. sugar
½ c. margarine
¼ c. nuts, chopped
½ tsp. ground cinnamon
1½ tsp. baking powder

½ tsp. baking soda
2 eggs, beaten
1 c. applesauce or apple butter
1 tsp. vanilla
½ c. raisins (opt.)

Make crumb mixture by combining ¾ cup flour and the sugar; cut in margarine. For topping, combine ½ cup crumb mixture with nuts and cinnamon. Set aside. To remaining crumb mixture add remaining flour, baking powder and baking soda. Add eggs, applesauce or apple butter and vanilla. Add raisins as desired. Beat until well blended. Pour into a greased 9 x 9 x 2-inch baking pan. Sprinkle topping on batter. Bake in a 375° oven for 30 to 35 minutes or until a toothpick inserted near the center comes out clean. Serve warm. Yield: 4 servings.

♥ YOU ARE MY SUNSHINE CAKE ♥

1½ c. whole-wheat flour
1 tsp. baking soda
1 T. orange zest
1½ c. orange juice concentrate

1 T. vinegar
1 tsp. vanilla
6 T. canola oil

Mix together flour, baking soda, orange zest and ½ cup orange juice concentrate. Make 3 indentations in batter then pour in vinegar, vanilla and oil. Pour remaining orange juice concentrate over batter and mix well. Coat 8-inch square baking pan with cooking spray and pour in batter. Bake at 350° for 30 minutes or until a toothpick inserted near the center comes out clean. Yield: 4 servings.

♥ GOTCHA GRANOLA ♥

6 c. oats
1/2 c. brown sugar
3/4 c. wheat germ
1 c. bran
1/2 c. sunflower seeds
1 c. nuts, chopped

1/2 c. dry nonfat milk
2/3 c. honey
2/3 c. oil
2 T. water
1 1/2 tsp. vanilla
1 1/2 c. raisins

In a large bowl combine oats, brown sugar, wheat germ, bran, sunflower seeds, nuts and dry milk. In another bowl mix honey, oil, water and vanilla. Add to dry mixture and stir. Place in large shallow pan. Bake in 300° oven for 25 to 30 minutes until lightly toasted, stirring occasionally. Remove from oven and cool, stirring occasionally. Add raisins. Store in tightly sealed container. Serve with milk or yogurt. Yield: 12 servings.

♥ SCRAMBLED EGGS ♥

6 eggs
1/3 c. milk
1/4 tsp. salt
Dash pepper

Diced vegetable, spices or cheese
  (opt.)
1 T. margarine

In a bowl beat together eggs, milk, salt and pepper. Mix in vegetables, cheeses, spices or any desired ingredient. Melt margarine in a large skillet over medium heat. Pour egg mixture in skillet. Cook, without stirring, until mixture begins to set on the bottom and around the edges. Using a large spoon or spatula, lift and fold partially cooked eggs so uncooked portion flows underneath. Continue to cook over medium heat for 2 to 3 minutes or until eggs are cooked through but are still glossy and moist. Immediately remove from heat and serve. Yield: 2 servings.

♥ SPICY SCRAMBLED EGGS ♥

2 tsp. vegetable oil
3 (6-inch) corn tortillas, cut into
  thin strips
1/4 c. onion, chopped

8 eggs, beaten
1 c. salsa
1/4 c. sour cream
2 T. green onions, chopped

Heat oil in 10-inch nonstick skillet over medium to high heat. Cook tortilla strips and onion in oil about 5 minutes, stirring frequently, until tortilla strips are crispy. Pour eggs over tortilla mixture. Reduce to medium heat. As mixture begins to set at bottom and side, gently lift cooked portions with spatula so uncooked portion will settle to bottom of skillet. Do not stir. Cook 4 to 5 minutes or until eggs are thick but moist. Top each serving with salsa, sour cream and green onions. Yield: 4 servings.

♥ EGG CUPS ♥

Bacon strips
Eggs
Milk
Butter

Salt and pepper to taste
Various seasonings to taste
Cheese slices

Preheat oven to 400°. Partially cook bacon and drain on paper towels. Spray cups of muffin pan with nonstick cooking spray. Line each cup with a strip of bacon and break 1 egg into each cup. Top each egg with 1 teaspoon milk, $\frac{1}{2}$ tsp. butter, salt, pepper and seasonings. Bake 15 to 20 minutes or until yolk is set. Add slice of cheese that has been cut to fit in muffin cup and cook about 2 minutes or until cheese is melted. Use a knife to pop eggs out of cups and serve. Yield: 2 eggs per person.

♥ APPLE SAUSAGE ♥

1 lb. link sausage
6 med. baking apples, pared and
 sliced

Salt and pepper to taste
1 T. lemon juice
3 T. brown sugar

Brown sausage and cut each link in half. Drain thoroughly and set aside. Butter a $1\frac{1}{2}$-quart casserole dish. Combine apples and sausage and put in casserole. Sprinkle with salt, pepper, lemon juice and brown sugar. Cover and bake at 350° for 45 minutes. Yield: 4 to 6 servings.

♥ LOVE GRITS ♥

1 lb. sausage, browned
Hot pepper sauce to taste
$\frac{1}{3}$ clove garlic, minced
$\frac{1}{2}$ tsp. salt
$\frac{1}{8}$ tsp. pepper
1 c. instant grits

2 c. boiling water
1 c. sharp Cheddar cheese, grated
$\frac{1}{4}$ c. butter, melted
2 lg. eggs, beaten
1 (8-oz.) can mild green chiles,
 seeded and chopped

Brown sausage and drain. Add hot sauce, garlic, salt and pepper. Mix and set aside. Cook grits in boiling water. Add all ingredients together, stirring until well mixed. Pour mixture into a well-buttered 9 x 13-inch baking dish. Bake uncovered at 350° for 1 hour. Yield: 8 servings.

♥ BREAKFAST FOR TWO ♥

1 (8-oz.) pkg. crabmeat
¼ c. mayonnaise
1 (3-oz.) pkg. cream cheese
1 egg yolk

1 tsp. onion, minced
¼ tsp. mustard, dry
1-2 dashes salt
2 English muffins, halved

Mix crabmeat, mayonnaise, cream cheese, egg yolk, onion, dry mustard and salt. Spread on the 4 halves of English muffins. Place under broiler until lightly browned. Yield: 2 servings.

♥ "EGGS"OTIC CASSEROLE ♥

2 c. plain croutons
1 c. Cheddar cheese, shredded
4 eggs
2 c. milk

½ tsp. salt
½ tsp. prepared mustard
⅛ tsp. onion or garlic powder
Dash pepper

Mix croutons and cheese in baking pan. In separate bowl combine eggs, milk, salt, mustard, onion or garlic powder and pepper. Mix with whisk until blended. Pour over croutons and cheese. Bake at 325° for 55 to 65 minutes. Yield: 2 servings.

♥ BREAFAST-IN-BED BAKED BREAKFAST ♥

1½ c. shoestring potatoes, canned
4 eggs
6 T. green onions
2 c. sharp Cheddar cheese

6 slices bacon, crumbled
2 T. parsley, chopped
½ c. tomato, chopped
Fresh basil

Spread potatoes in bottom of 10-inch pie pan. Make 4 holes in bottom of mixture and put one egg in each hole. Bake at 350° for 10 to 12 minutes or until eggs are set. Sprinkle on onions, cheese, bacon and parsley and bake 3 or 4 minutes longer. Cut in 4 wedges. Sprinkle top with tomato and basil. Yield: 4 regular or 2 generous servings.

"The critical period in matrimony is breakfast-time."
--Sir Alan Patrick Herbert

♥ BREAKFAST PIZZA ♥

1 (8-oz.) can crescent rolls
1 lb. sausage
1 c. frozen hash browns, thawed
Onion flakes
Green pepper, chopped

1 c. Cheddar cheese, shredded
5 eggs
¼ c. milk
Salt and pepper to taste

Spread rolls onto 12 to 14-inch pizza pan. Brown sausage and put on dough. Add hash browns, onions, peppers and part of the cheese. In separate bowl mix eggs, milk, salt and pepper. Pour over hash browns. Sprinkle with remaining cheese. Bake at 375° for 30 minutes. Yield: 4 servings.

♥ BREAKFAST IN BED BURRITO ♥

1 lb. sausage, ground
4 eggs, beaten
1 onion, chopped
1 bell pepper, chopped

Flour tortillas
Salsa
Cheddar cheese, shredded

Fry and drain sausage. Mix together eggs, onion and peppers and scramble. Mix with sausage. Fill tortillas with mixture, salsa and cheese. Fold ends inside and roll. Yield: 4 servings.

♥ KISS ME QUICHE ♥

1 c. Swiss cheese, grated
8-10 slices bacon, cooked crisp and
  crumbled
¼ c. onion, minced
1 (10-oz.) pkg. frozen chopped
  spinach
½ tsp. salt

4 eggs
1 (14-oz.) ctn. small curd cottage
  cheese
½ tsp. pepper
1 tsp. Worcestershire sauce
3 drops hot pepper sauce

Sprinkle cheese, bacon and onion in a 10-inch greased pie plate. Boil spinach with salt and drain. Beat spinach and remaining ingredients together until well blended. Pour over the bacon mixture. Bake at 350° for 35 to 40 minutes. Cool 15 minutes before serving so mixture will set. Yield: 6 to 8 servings.

"Love consists in this, that two solitudes protect and touch and greet each other."

--Ranier Maria Rilke

♥ CRUSTLESS QUICHE ♥

¼ lb. butter
½ c. flour
6 eggs
1 c. milk
1 lb. Monterey Jack cheese, cubed
1 (3-oz.) pkg. cream cheese,
  softened

2 c. cottage cheese
1 tsp. baking powder
1 tsp. salt
1 tsp. sugar

Melt butter in small saucepan. Add flour and cook until smooth. Set aside. Beat eggs. Add milk, cheeses, baking powder, salt, sugar and butter-flour mixture to eggs. Stir until well blended. Pour mixture into a well greased 9 x 13 x 2-inch pan. Bake uncovered at 350° for 45 minutes. Cut and serve. Yield: 6 to 8 servings.

♥ QUICHE OF LOVE ♥

2 c. zucchini and/or summer
  squash, thinly sliced
1 c. onion, chopped
½ c. fresh mushrooms, sliced
½ c. red sweet pepper, chopped
1 T. margarine
¼ c. fresh or 1 T. dried parsley
2 T. fresh or 1 tsp. dried basil,
  crushed

¼ tsp. garlic powder
1 T. fresh or 1¼ tsp. dried
  oregano, crushed
⅛ tsp. pepper
2 eggs, beaten
1 c. ham, cooked and diced
1 c. mozzarella cheese, shredded
½ c. Fontina cheese, shredded
1 (8-roll) pkg. refrigerated biscuits

In large skillet cook zucchini and/or squash, onion, mushrooms and sweet pepper in hot margarine for about 6 minutes or just until tender, stirring occasionally. Remove from heat. Stir in parsley, basil, garlic powder, oregano and pepper. Stir in eggs, ham, mozzarella and Fontina cheese. Set mixture aside. Arrange 7 slightly flattened biscuits around edge of a greased 10-inch quiche dish, allowing dough to extend over side. Place remaining biscuit in bottom of dish. Pinch edges together to seal. Flatten slightly to form a crust. Evenly spread filling over the crust. Bake in a 375° oven for about 25 minutes or until a knife inserted near the center comes out clean. Cover the edge with foil the last 5 to 10 minutes. Garnish with additional fresh basil as desired. Yield: 8 servings.

♥ ITALIAN HONEYMOON OMELET ♥

8 eggs, beaten
1 c. ricotta cheese
1/2 c. milk
1/2 tsp. dried basil, crushed
1/4 tsp. salt
1/4 tsp. fennel seed, crushed
1/4 tsp. pepper

1 (10-oz.) pkg. frozen chopped
  spinach, thawed and drained
1 c. tomato, chopped
1 c. mozzarella cheese, shredded
1/2 c. green onion, thinly sliced
1/2 c. salami, diced

In large mixing bowl combine eggs and ricotta cheese and beat just until combined. Stir in milk, basil, salt, fennel and pepper. Fold in spinach, tomatoes, mozzarella, green onion and salami. Spread evenly in a greased 3-quart rectangular baking dish. Bake in a 325° oven for 30 to 35 minutes or until a knife inserted near the center comes out clean. Let stand for 10 minutes before serving. Yield: 6 to 8 servings.

♥ SWISS CHEESE OMELET ♥

3 T. butter
1 small onion, chopped
1 (4-oz.) can sliced mushrooms,
  drained

6 eggs
1/4 c. Italian dressing
2 T. water
1/2 c. Swiss cheese, shredded

In skillet melt 2 tablespoons butter and sauté onion and mushrooms until golden. Beat together eggs, Italian dressing, water and Swiss cheese. Pour egg mixture over onion and mushroom mixture in skillet. It should set at edges at once. Reduce heat slightly and using a fork, lift cooked portions at edges so uncooked egg mixture settles to the bottom of pan. Add remaining butter and rapidly slide pan back and forth over moderate heat until mixture sets but surface is still moist. Increase heat to brown bottom quickly. Fold in half and roll out onto heated platter. Yield: 2 servings.

♥ OMELET OF HAPPINESS ♥

4 slices bacon
2 c. raw potato, shredded
1/4 c. onion, chopped
1/4 c. green pepper, chopped

4 eggs
1/4 c. milk
Salt and pepper to taste
Cheddar cheese, shredded

Fry bacon until crisp. Remove bacon, drain and crumble, leaving drippings in frying pan. In same pan mix potatoes, onion and pepper. Cook over low heat until contents are crisp and brown. Blend eggs and milk and pour over potatoes. Top mixture with cheese and bacon. Cover and cook about 10 minutes. Loosen mixture with spatula and serve. Yield: 2 servings.

♥ HEARTY SAUSAGE GRAVY ♥

1 lb. sage-flavored sausage, ground
2 T. onion, chopped
6 T. flour
1 qt. milk

½ tsp. poultry seasoning
¼ tsp. salt
Dash Worcestershire sauce
Dash hot pepper sauce

Brown sausage in large frying pan. Add onion. Continue cooking until onion is soft and transparent. Drain all drippings except 2 tablespoons and return to frying pan. Combine remaining ingredients in large bowl and mix well with wire whisk. Add to sausage and onions. Cook, stirring frequently, until thick. Serve over biscuits. Yield: 6 to 8 servings.

♥ BAKING POWDER BISCUITS ♥

2 c. flour
½ tsp. salt
2 tsp. sugar
4 tsp. baking powder

½ tsp. cream of tartar
½ c. butter
⅔ c. milk

Preheat oven to 425°. Sift flour, salt, sugar, baking powder and cream of tartar together. Cut in butter until mixture resembles coarse sand. Pour milk over the mixture. Stir with a fork until dough "follows" the fork around the bowl. Pat the dough out on a countertop or board until it is ¾-inch thick. Cut dough with a plain round cookie cutter of desired diameter. Place on ungreased cookie sheet and bake for 12 to 14 minutes or until golden brown. Yield: approximately 1 dozen biscuits.

When our two souls stand up
erect and strong,
Face to face, silent, drawing
nigh and nigher,
Until the lengthening wings
break into fire
At either curved point,--
what bitter wrong
Can the earth do to us,
that we should not long
Be here contented?
--Elizabeth Barrett Browning

BEFORE
THINGS
GET COOKING

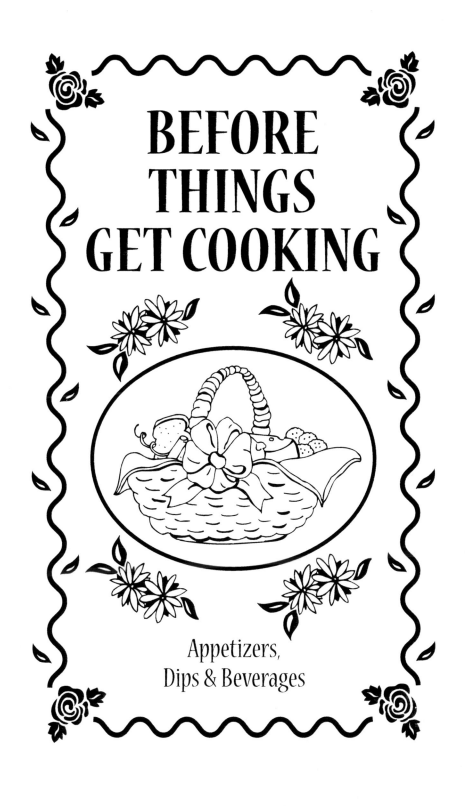

Appetizers,
Dips & Beverages

Useful Utensils
Finding the right tools to get you started in the kitchen

If you have generous friends and relatives, you might have everything necessary to prepare a decent supper. But if you want to create some real culinary delights, or even a simple well-balanced meal, you may need to invest in a few pieces of additional kitchenware.

Though all aren't absolutely necessary, many homes run more smoothly with a microwave, toaster, blender, coffee pot, electric mixer, food processor, crock pot, electric skillet and deep fat fryer. Most cooks already have needed daily items like flatware, glassware, pots, pans and place settings. Still, there are other items you may or may not have considered purchasing. The following list is divided into categories of things you will probably use on a daily basis, items you might need once in a while, and things that aren't necessary but may be nice to have around.

Must Haves
Baking dishes
   7 x 11-inch pan
   9 x 13-inch pan
   8 x 8-inch pan
   2-quart covered
   casserole dish
Basic set of knives
   paring, chef, serrated
   and carving
Canisters
Can opener
Cheese grater
Colander
Cookie sheet
Cutting board
Hot pads
Kitchen shears
Measuring cups
   and spoons
Mixing bowls
Muffin tin
Pancake turner

Plastic storage containers and lids
Rubber scraper
Spatula
Stockpot
Vegetable peeler
Wire whisk
Wooden spoons

Should Haves
Garlic press
Gravy boat and ladle
Juicer
Lasagna pan
Microwave cookware
9 x 5-inch loaf pan
Pastry brush
Pie plate
Pizza cutter
Rolling pin
Salad tongs
Soup ladle

Sugar and creamer set
Steamer
Tea pot
Thermometer
Timer

Future Aspirations
Apple corer
Cooking stone
Custard cups
Griddle
Knife sharpener
Pastry scraper
Salad spinner
Serving platters
Souffle dish
Waffle iron
Wok

Before Things Get Cooking

Darling Dips & Spreads

♥ GUACAMOLE TO DIE FOR ♥

2 med. avocados, seeded, peeled
  and diced
$\frac{1}{2}$ small onion, diced
$\frac{1}{4}$ c. green chili peppers, diced
1 T. parsley
1 T. lemon juice

1 clove garlic, minced
$\frac{1}{4}$ tsp. salt
1 med. tomato, peeled and finely
  chopped (opt.)
Tortilla chips

In a blender or food processor combine avocado, onion, chili peppers, parsley, lemon juice, garlic and salt. Cover and blend until mixture is smooth, scraping sides of bowl as necessary. Stir in tomato, if desired. Transfer to serving bowl, cover and chill for 24 hours before serving with tortilla chips. Yield: 6 to 8 servings with other appetizers, 4 if only appetizer served.

♥ VEGETABLE DIP ♥

1 (3-oz.) pkg. cream cheese
1 tsp. lemon juice
1 pkg. dry Italian dressing mix

1 c. sour cream
Favorite vegetable sticks

Soften cream cheese. Add lemon juice and beat well. Add dressing mix and sour cream and beat. Refrigerate overnight and serve with desired vegetables. Yield: 4 to 8 servings.

♥ CUPID'S DIP ♥

¼ c. sugar
¼ c. cornstarch
¼ tsp. salt
1 c. pineapple juice
¼ c. orange juice
2 T. lemon juice

2 eggs, beaten
2 T. grenadine syrup
1 (8-oz.) pkg. cream cheese,
  softened
Assorted fruit as desired

Mix sugar, cornstarch and salt in saucepan. Add pineapple, orange and lemon juices. Heat and stir in eggs and grenadine until mixture boils and thickens. Add cream cheese in small pieces. Whisk or beat until melted and smooth. Chill and serve with desired fruit. Yield: 8 servings.

♥ CHILI & CHEESE DIP ♥

1 lb. hamburger, browned and
  drained
1 (8-oz.) jar processed cheese
  spread

1 (15-oz.) can beanless chili
Corn chips

Mix together and heat all ingredients. Keep warm in small crockpot. Serve with corn chips. Yield: 8 servings.

♥ COME BACK FOR MORE DIP ♥

3 c. cottage cheese
¾ c. plain yogurt
¾ c. green onions, sliced

1 red bell pepper, chopped
1 (1¼-oz.) pkg. taco seasoning mix
½ tsp. red pepper

In a blender or food processor process cottage cheese just until curds are smoothed out but not runny. In a large bowl combine all ingredients until well mixed. Cover and chill 2 hours. Yield: 8 to 12 servings.

"Married couples who love each other tell each other a thousand things without talking."

--Chinese Proverb

BRIDE-06

♥ TACO SALAD DIP ♥

½ lb. ground beef
1 (16-oz.) can refried beans
1 (8-oz.) can tomato sauce
1 (1¼-oz.) pkg. taco seasoning mix
¼ c. onion, chopped fine
¼ c. green bell pepper, chopped
  fine
2-3 drops red pepper sauce

1 small clove garlic, chopped fine
½ c. sour cream
1 T. pasteurized processed cheese,
  grated
⅛ tsp. chili powder
Lettuce, finely shredded
Cheddar cheese, shredded
Tortilla chips

Crumble ground beef in 1½-quart microwavable casserole. Cover loosely and microwave on high 2½ to 3½ minutes or until very little pink remains. Stir and drain. Stir in beans, tomato sauce, taco seasoning mix, onion, bell pepper, pepper sauce and garlic. Cover tightly and microwave 3 minutes before stirring. Spread in microwavable 9 x 1¼-inch pie plate. Cover and microwave on high 3 to 4 minutes or until hot and bubbly. In separate dish mix sour cream, American cheese and chili powder. Mound sour cream mixture on top of beef mixture. Sprinkle with lettuce and cheese. Serve with tortilla chips. Yield: 8 servings.

♥ DRIED BEEF DIP ♥

1 c. sour cream
1 c. mayonnaise or salad dressing
1 tsp. prepared horseradish
¼ tsp. dried dill weed

1 (2½-oz.) pkg. dried beef, finely
  chopped
Chips or raw vegetables

Mix all ingredients except beef until smooth. Stir in beef. Serve with chips or raw vegetables. Yield: 8 servings.

"What love is, if thou wouldst be taught,
Thy heart must teach alone--
Two souls with but a single thought,
Two hearts that beat as one."

--Friedrich Halm

♥ EIGHT-LAYER SPREAD ♥

1 (8¼-oz.) can refried beans
¼ c. picante or taco sauce
1 c. lettuce, shredded
1 (8-oz.) ctn. sour cream
1 (6-oz.) ctn. frozen avocado dip,
  thawed
1 c. Monterey Jack or Cheddar
  cheese, shredded

¼ c. green onion, sliced
2 T. pitted ripe olives, sliced or
  chopped
2 med. tomatoes, chopped
Tortilla chips or crackers

Stir together beans and picante or taco sauce. Arrange lettuce on a 12-inch platter, leaving a 2-inch open rim at edge of platter. Spread bean mixture over lettuce, making a layer about ¼-inch thick. Then, layer sour cream and avocado dip. Top with cheese, onion, olives and tomatoes. Cover and chill up to 24 hours. Arrange chips on platter around dip and spread as desired. Yield: 10 to 12 servings.

♥ BEER CHEESE SPREAD ♥

1 (8-oz.) pkg. cream cheese
1 (4-oz.) pkg. processed sharp
  Cheddar cheese
1 T. green onion tops, chopped

⅓ c. beer
1 tsp. horseradish
½ tsp. dry mustard
Crackers or vegetables

Melt cheeses in a glass dish in microwave for 2½ minutes. Gradually beat in remaining ingredients. Cook covered for 2 minutes, stirring twice. Serve hot or cold with crackers or vegetables. Yield: 8 servings.

♥ PECAN SPREAD ♥

1 (8-oz.) pkg. cream cheese
2 T. milk
¼ c. green pepper, finely chopped
½ tsp. garlic salt
¼ tsp. pepper
2 T. dry onion flakes

½ c. sour cream
1 T. butter
½ c. pecans, coarsely chopped
½ tsp. salt
Crackers or chips

Put cream cheese in small casserole dish suitable for serving. Microwave for 45 seconds or just until softened. Add milk, green pepper, garlic salt, pepper, onion flakes and sour cream. Mix well. Place butter in a cup and microwave for 30 seconds to melt. Add nuts and salt to melted butter. Stir well and drain on paper towel. Spoon nuts over cheese mixture. Serve hot or cold with crackers or chips. Yield: 2 cups.

Appealing Appetizers

♥ SAUCY SHRIMP COCKTAIL ♥

1 lb. fresh or frozen peeled shrimp,
  cooked, deveined and chilled
Lettuce

Cocktail sauce
Lemon wedges

Arrange shrimp in six lettuce-lined cocktail cups or glasses. Spoon 1 tablespoon cocktail sauce over each cup. Serve with lemon. Yield: 6 servings.

♥ STEAMY STUFFED MUSHROOMS ♥

1 lb. fresh mushrooms
1 garlic clove, chopped
1 egg
1 T. Parmesan cheese, grated

$1/4$ tsp. pepper
1 tsp. onion, grated
1 tsp. parsley flakes
$1/2$ tsp. salt

Clean mushrooms. Twist out stems and chop the stems finely. Mix together stems with rest of ingredients. Fill cavity of mushroom with mixture. Put on cookie sheet and bake at 350° for 25 minutes. Yield: 6 servings.

♥ CHEESY TORTILLA HUGS ♥

1 (8-oz.) pkg. cream cheese
1 (8-oz.) ctn. sour cream
1 bunch green onions, finely
  chopped
1 c. ripe olives, chopped

1 (4-oz.) can green chilies, chopped
1 tsp. cumin
$1/2$ tsp. chili powder
Flour tortillas
Picante sauce

Soften cream cheese. Add sour cream and mix well. Add onions, olives, chilies and spices. Spread about $1/3$ cup mixture on each tortilla. Roll up tightly. Place in sealed container and chill at least 4 hours. Cut into slices. Arrange on platter around a bowl of picante sauce. Yield: 10 to 12 servings.

"What is a kiss? Why this, as some approve;
The sure, sweet cement, glue, and lime of love."
--Robert Herrick

♥ NACHOS SUPREME ♥

½ c. water
2 lbs. pasteurized processed cheese,
 cubed
1 (16-oz.) jar salsa
1 lb. ground beef, browned and
 drained

Tortilla chips
Black olives (opt.)
Green onion, chopped (opt.)
Tomato, diced (opt.)

Place water in slow cooker and turn it on high. Add cheese when water is hot. When cheese is melted, add salsa and stir before adding meat. Cook mixture on low heat for 30 minutes. Serve with plain tortilla chips. Garnish with black olives, chopped green onion and tomatoes, if desired. Yield: 12 servings.

♥ SPICY LOVE QUICHE ♥

1 (4-oz.) can green chilies, chopped
 and drained
2 c. Monterey Jack or Cheddar
 cheese, shredded

1 c. baking mix
1 c. half-and-half
4 eggs
⅛ tsp. red pepper sauce (opt.)

Heat oven to 375°. Grease 9 x 9 x 2-inch square pan. Sprinkle chilies and cheese in pan. Beat remaining ingredients with hand beater for 1 minute or 15 seconds in blender on high speed until smooth. Pour mixture into pan. Bake about 30 minutes or until golden brown and knife inserted in center comes out clean. Let stand 10 minutes before cutting into squares. Yield: 32 squares.

♥ MEXICAN QUICHE APPETIZER ♥

½ c. butter
10 eggs
½ c. flour
1 tsp. baking powder
Dash salt

1 (8-to 12-oz.) can mild green
 chilies, chopped
2 c. cottage cheese
4 c. Monterey Jack cheese, grated

Melt butter in 9 x 13-inch baking pan; set aside. In a large mixing bowl beat eggs and add flour, baking powder and salt; mix well. Add melted butter to egg mixture. Add chilies and cheeses. Mix together and pour into baking pan. Bake uncovered at 350° for 45 to 60 minutes or until knife inserted in center comes out clean. Cut into squares while hot but cool slightly before removing from pan. Yield: 24 servings.

♥ GOTCHA GREEN CHILE BITES ♥

Butter
1 (4-oz.) can mild green chiles, chopped

4 c. sharp Cheddar cheese, grated
6 eggs, beaten

Butter bottom of an 8 x 8-inch baking pan. Spread green chiles on bottom of pan. Sprinkle grated cheese over chilies and pour eggs over all. Bake uncovered at 350° for 30 minutes or until mixture remains firm when pan is shaken. Cut into squares and serve hot. Yield: 64 small pieces or 32 generous pieces.

♥ SASSY SPINACH AND CHEESE SQUARES ♥

½ c. butter
3 eggs
1 c. flour
1 c. milk
1 tsp. salt

1 tsp. baking powder
4 c. Monterey Jack cheese, grated
4 c. fresh spinach, chopped
⅛ tsp. cayenne pepper or ¼ tsp. hot sauce

Melt butter in 9 x 13-inch pan. Beat eggs. Add flour, milk, salt and baking powder. Add cheese, spinach and pepper or hot sauce. Mix well. Spread into pan and bake at 350° for 35 minutes. Cool 30 minutes and cut into squares before serving. Yield: 40 squares.

♥ AREN'T YOU CUTE ARTICHOKE ♥ SQUARES

2 (6-oz.) jars marinated artichoke hearts
1 sm. onion, finely chopped
4 eggs
¼ c. dry bread crumbs, fine
⅛ tsp. pepper

⅛ tsp. oregano
¼ tsp. salt
2 T. parsley, chopped
⅛ tsp. hot pepper sauce
2 c. Cheddar cheese, grated

Drain artichokes, saving marinade from 1 jar. Sauté onion in marinade. Cut up artichokes. Beat eggs and add crumbs and seasonings to egg mixture. Stir in remaining ingredients. Turn all into a greased 7 x 11-inch pan. Bake at 325° for 30 minutes. Let cool before cutting into squares. Serve hot or cold. Yield: 40 squares.

♥ CHICKEN WINGS ♥

1½ lbs. chicken wings (about 8)
½ c. ketchup
¼ c. onion, chopped fine

1 T. honey
1 T. vinegar
1 clove garlic, minced

Rinse chicken and pat dry. Cut off and discard wing tips. Cut each wing at joint to make 2 sections. Place wing pieces in a single layer in 13 x 9 x 2-inch baking pan. Bake in 375° oven for 20 minutes. Drain fat from baking pan. For sauce, combine remaining ingredients. Brush wings with sauce. Bake 10 minutes. Turn wings over and brush again with sauce. Bake an additional 5 to 10 minutes or until chicken is tender. Yield: 16 servings.

♥ EASY POTATO SKINS ♥

12 med. baking potatoes
½ c. margarine
2 c. Cheddar or Monterey Jack
  cheese, shredded

Garlic or seasoned salt (opt.)
Salsa
Green onion, sliced

Prick potatoes with a fork and bake in a 425° oven for 40 to 50 minutes or until tender. Cut lengthwise into quarters. Scoop out the insides (reserving insides for another use if desired), leaving ½-inch thick shells. Brush both sides of potato skins with margarine. Place, cut side up, on a large baking sheet. Bake at 425° for 10 to 15 minutes or until crisp. Sprinkle with cheese and salt as desired. Bake about 2 minutes more or until cheese melts. Serve with salsa and green onion. Yield: 48 skins.

♥ ZESTY CINNAMON STICKS ♥

2 lg. sweet potatoes
1 T. canola or safflower oil

Ground cinnamon

Scrub and peel potatoes. Cut into strips as for French fries. Toss with oil and sprinkle with cinnamon to taste. Spread onto a non-stick baking sheet. Bake at 350° for 10 to 15 minutes or until soft. Yield: 4 servings.

"To get the full value of joy, you must have someone to divide it with."

--Mark Twain

♥ POTATO PUFFS ♥

½ c. water
½ c. milk
2 T. margarine
½ tsp. salt

1⅓ c. instant mashed potatoes
2 eggs, beaten
Vegetable oil

Boil water, milk, margarine and salt in a 2-quart saucepan and remove from heat. Stir in instant mashed potatoes until stiff. Cool and stir in eggs. Drop potato mixture by teaspoonfuls onto cookie sheet covered with waxed paper. Refrigerate at least 2 hours before forming into balls. Heat ½-inch oil in a 10-inch skillet until hot. Drop potato balls into hot oil and fry over medium-high heat for 1½ to 2 minutes on each side, or until puff is golden brown. To prepare puffs immediately, drop potato mixture by teaspoonfuls directly into hot oil without refrigerating. Fry as directed above. Yield: 4 servings.

♥ ONION-CHEESE PUFFS ♥

1 c. water
⅓ c. margarine
1 c. all-purpose flour
1 tsp. salt

¼ tsp. garlic powder
4 eggs
¾ c. Swiss cheese, shredded
¼ c. onion, chopped

Heat oven to 400°. Grease cookie sheet lightly. Heat water and margarine to rolling boil in 2-quart saucepan. Stir in flour, salt and garlic powder. Stir vigorously over low heat for 1 minute or until mixture forms a ball. Remove from heat. Beat in eggs until smooth. Stir in cheese and onion. Drop dough by scant teaspoonfuls about 1 inch apart onto cookie sheet. Bake 20 to 25 minutes or until puffed and golden. Serve warm. Yield: 4 servings.

"When I write of hunger, I am really writing about love and the hunger for it, and warmth and the love of it and the hunger for it...and then the warmth and richness and fine reality of hunger satisfied...and it is all one."
--M.F.K. Fisher

♥ DON'T BE A CRAB PUFFS ♥

²/₃ c. water
1¹/₃ c. pie crust mix
1 T. all-purpose flour
4 eggs
1 (8-oz.) pkg. cream cheese,
  softened

1 (6-oz.) pkg. frozen crabmeat,
  thawed and drained
¹/₃ c. chutney
¹/₄ c. green onions with tops, sliced
¹/₄ tsp. curry powder

Heat oven to 400°. In 2-quart saucepan heat water to boiling. Stir in pie crust mix and flour. Stir vigorously over medium heat until mixture forms a ball and leaves side of pan. Remove from heat. With electric mixer beat in eggs, one at a time, on medium speed until mixture is thick and shiny. Drop mixture by rounded teaspoonfuls onto ungreased cookie sheet. Bake 13 to 15 minutes or until puffed and golden. Cool on wire rack away from draft. Cut puffs in half. Thoroughly mix cream cheese, crabmeat, chutney, onions and curry powder. Fill each puff with scant tablespoon crab filling. Refrigerate before serving. Yield: 4 servings.

Beverages

♥ CUDDLE-UP CAPPUCCINO MIX ♥

1 c. instant coffee creamer
1 c. instant chocolate drink mix
²/₃ c. instant coffee crystals

¹/₂ c. sugar
¹/₂ tsp. cinnamon
¹/₄ tsp. nutmeg

Combine all ingredients and mix well. Store in container with a tight lid. To prepare 1 serving, add 3 tablespoons mix to 6 ounces hot water and stir well. Yield: 3 cups dry mix.

♥ MOCHA SNUGGLER ♥

2¹/₂ c. powdered nondairy creamer
2 c. hot cocoa mix
1 c. instant coffee crystals
1 c. instant chocolate drink mix

¹/₄ c. sugar
2 tsp. ground cinnamon
¹/₂ tsp. ground nutmeg

Combine all ingredients and mix well. Store in an airtight container. To serve, add 1 tablespoon mix to ³/₄ cup boiling water. You can use all "lite" ingredients. Yield: 6³/₄ cups dry mix.

♥ HOT APPLE CIDER ♥

1 (1-gal.) bottle apple cider or juice
10 oz. brown sugar

2 tsp. cinnamon
½ pat butter per 6 oz. cider

Mix cider, sugar and cinnamon and heat in crockpot. Add ½ pat butter per 6 ounces cider. Stir and enjoy. Yield: 20 (6-ounce) servings.

♥ SPICED APPLE CIDER ♥

3 qts. apple cider
10 whole allspice
10 sticks cinnamon
12 whole cloves

3 sm. pieces ginger or 1 T. candied
  ginger
¾ c. brown sugar, packed

Bring all ingredients except sugar to a boil. Stir in sugar and simmer 15 minutes. Strain and serve hot. Yield: 16 (6-ounce) servings.

♥ COLD WINTER'S NIGHT COCOA MIX ♥

3 c. powdered milk
¾ c. sugar
½ c. cocoa
Dash salt

Boiling water
1 oz. Peppermint Schnapps (opt.)
Whipped cream (opt.)

Sift together milk, sugar, cocoa and salt. For each serving, mix 8 ounces boiling water with 4 tablespoons mix. Add Peppermint Schnapps and whipped cream as desired. Yield: 8 (8-ounce) servings.

♥ HOT TODDYS ♥

3 sticks cinnamon
2 tsp. whole cloves
½ tsp. ground nutmeg
½ gal. apple cider

1 c. sugar
2 c. orange juice
½ c. lemon juice
1 c. brandy, any fruit flavor

Tie cinnamon, cloves and nutmeg in cheesecloth. Simmer cider and sugar with spices for about 15 minutes. Remove bag of seasonings. Add orange juice, lemon juice and brandy. Heat to bubbling and serve. Yield: 3 quarts = 12 (8-ounce) servings.

♥ CHAMPAGNE MIMOSAS ♥

Orange juice
Champagne

Fruit slices (opt.)

Fill champagne flute with orange juice until half full and finish filling with champagne. Garnish with slice of orange or other fruit placed on rim of glass.

♥ SOOTHING ALMOND TEA ♥

3 tea bags
6 c. water
1 c. sugar

⅔ c. lemon juice
2 tsp. almond extract
1 tsp. vanilla extract

Steep tea bags in 2 cups boiling water for 10 minutes. Boil sugar in 4 cups water for 5 minutes and then add lemon juice and flavorings. Combine the liquids and heat. Serve hot or cold. Yield: 7 cups.

♥ GOLDEN BAND PUNCH ♥

2 c. sugar
2 c. water
2 c. lemon juice
2 c. orange juice

4 (1 ltr.) bottles ginger ale, chilled
Vodka (opt.)

Mix concentrate of sugar, water and juices. Divide into 4 pint jars. This can be done days in advance and stored in refrigerator. Mix 1 pint of concentrate with 1 bottle ginger ale just before serving. Vodka can also be added for a different flavor. Each pint makes 1½ quarts when mixed. Yield: 4 pints.

♥ SUMMER COOLER ♥

1 (6-oz.) can frozen lemonade
⅓ c. grenadine syrup
1 tsp. almond flavoring

2 qts. iced tea
Lemon and cherry slices (opt.)

Add lemonade to syrup. Stir in flavoring and tea. Pour into tall glasses with ice and garnish with lemon slices or cherries. Yield: 8 tall glasses.

♥ EASY PEACH SHAKE ♥

1 (16-oz.) can peaches in juice
1 pt. vanilla yogurt

Ice

Pour peaches with juice and yogurt into a blender. Add ice and blend until mixture is slushy. Pour into glasses. Yield: 2 servings.

♥ GONE BANANAS & CHOCOLATE SHAKE ♥

2 c. milk
1 ripe banana

4 T. sweetened cocoa
6 ice cubes

Combine all ingredients in blender. Cover tightly and blend until smooth. Pour into glasses and serve. Yield: 2 servings.

♥ MAGICAL MOCHA COOLER ♥

1 c. cold water
1 pt. chocolate ice cream
2 tsp. instant coffee crystals
1 tsp. vanilla

½ tsp. ground cinnamon
Sweetened whipped cream (opt.)
Cocoa (opt.)
Cinnamon sticks (opt.)

Place water, ice cream, instant coffee, vanilla and cinnamon in blender. Cover and blend until smooth on medium speed for 10 to 15 seconds, stopping occasionally to scrape sides of bowl. Pour into glasses and garnish with sweetened whipped cream dusted with cocoa and a cinnamon stick, if desired. Yield: 2 servings.

To My Dear and Loving Husband
If ever two were one, then surely we.
If ever man were loved by wife, then thee;
If ever wife was happy in a man,
Compare with me, ye women, if you can.
I prize thy love more than whole mines of gold
Or all the riches that the East doth hold.
My love is such that rivers cannot quench,
Nor ought but love from thee, give recompense.
Thy love is such I can no way repay,
The heavens reward thee manifold, I pray.
Then while we live, in love let's so perservere
That when we live no more, we may live ever.
                                        --Anne Bradstreet

Our Favorite Recipes

LOVIN'
from the
OVEN

Baked Goods

Cutting Culinary Costs

*Shopping and cooking
for less money*

After recovering from the shock of wedding and honeymoon bills, you may be tempted to begin a starvation diet to make ends meet. Instead of wasting away, the budget conscious bride can employ a little creativity to come up with some yummy meals that won't break the bank.

- Don't be too proud to clip coupons. Stretch dinner dollars as far as they can go by taking advantage of double coupon days at your local grocery store. When you find a good deal, stock up on canned items you know you'll use.
- For dishes calling for bread, like homemade dressing, spiced croutons or bread pudding, go to a bread thrift store or ask your friendly neighborhood baker for some day-old goods. The day-old stuff is still edible and usually has a nice discount.
- It's a good idea to invest in a few versatile plastic containers and lids. With airtight containers, you can keep your leftovers fresh in the freezer until you think of a way to recycle them. Many foods can be frozen for a second appearance, but try to be conservative in your estimates so you have fewer leftovers to work with in the future.
- To keep expensive impulse buying to a minimum, make a complete shopping list and stick to it. Remember it's not always necessary to buy brand names; generic brands are usually just as good and cost less. Compare prices and sizes to get the best deals. You may even try warehouses or bulk supply stores for items you use in greater quantities.
- Growing an herb garden is a wonderful way to reduce your spice budget Many great chefs use nothing but fresh herbs and spices because of their strong flavors. If you're short on green thumbs, buy spices and herbs in bulk and store them in your own containers to cut costs.
- Find creative ways to cook. Instead of using extra oil to fry chicken, steam, bake or broil it for a healthier and cheaper alternative. Instead of buying prepackaged frosting or gravy, concoct your own favorites to save a dime or two.
- If you can't afford meat, which can be one of the most expensive items on a shopping list, use beans, peas and eggs to provide the same nutrients. Or, make your meat give more bang for your buck by using it in casseroles and soups. Cut costs by serving less meat and more potatoes, rice, pastas, breads and other economical and filling foods.

Lovin' From The Oven

♥ COCOA LOVE LOAF ♥

²/₃ c. milk
½ c. warm water
2½ tsp. (1 pkg.) dry yeast
⅓ c. soft butter
½ c. dark brown sugar

½ tsp. salt
4 T. cocoa
2½ c. flour
²/₃ c. walnuts, broken
Cream cheese (opt.)

Scald milk and set aside to cool until lukewarm. Mix warm water and milk together and add yeast to mixture. Cream together butter, sugar, salt and cocoa. Add yeast mixture and stir well. Gradually add flour to make a soft dough that's just firm enough to knead. Knead in walnuts. Cover in a greased bowl and let mixture rise until double in size. Turn out and punch down. Place dough in greased 5 x 8-inch loaf pan. Let rise to double in size. Bake at 350° for 50 to 60 minutes. Toast and spread with cream cheese as desired. Yield: 6 to 8 servings.

♥ YOU ARE MY HONEY BREAD ♥

1 c. honey
1 c. milk
1 c. brown sugar, firmly packed
2 tsp. cinnamon
1 tsp. baking soda

½ tsp. salt
3½ c. flour
Cream cheese (opt.)
Orange marmalade (opt.)

Beat honey, milk and brown sugar until well blended. Mix together dry ingredients and add to honey mixture until well mixed. Pour into a well-greased 5 x 9-inch loaf pan and bake at 250° for 2½ hours or until toothpick inserted in center comes out clean. Toast and serve with cream cheese and orange marmalade as desired. Yield: 6 to 8 servings.

♥ CARAMEL PECAN PASSION ♥

¹/₃ c. caramel ice cream topping
2 T. butter, melted

¹/₃ c. pecan halves
1 (8-stick) pkg. refrigerator
   breadsticks

In a 9-inch round cake pan stir together caramel topping and butter. Sprinkle with pecans. Separate but don't uncoil breadsticks. Arrange breadstick coils on top of caramel mixture. Bake at 350° for 20 to 25 minutes or until golden brown. Let stand 2 to 3 minutes. Loosen sides and invert rolls onto plate. Serve warm. Yield: 8 servings.

♥ POUND CAKE MUFFINS ♥

2 c. all-purpose flour
3 tsp. poppy seeds
¹/₂ tsp. salt
¹/₄ tsp. baking soda
1 c. sugar

¹/₂ c. butter
2 eggs
1 c. plain yogurt
1 tsp. vanilla extract

In small bowl stir together flour, poppy seeds, salt and baking soda. In large bowl cream together sugar and butter. Beat in eggs one at a time. Beat in yogurt and vanilla until well blended. Stir in flour mixture until moistened thoroughly. Spoon batter into greased muffin tins and bake at 400° for 15 to 20 minutes or until a wooden toothpick inserted into center comes out clean. Cool muffins on wire rack for 5 minutes before serving. Yield: 1 dozen muffins.

♥ RASPBERRY MUFFINS ♥

1¹/₂ c. all-purpose flour
¹/₂ tsp. baking soda
¹/₂ tsp. salt
1¹/₂ tsp. ground cinnamon
1 c. sugar

1 (12-oz.) pkg. frozen unsweetened
   raspberries, thawed
2 eggs, well beaten
²/₃ c. vegetable oil
¹/₂ c. pecans, chopped

Preheat oven to 400°. In medium bowl mix flour, soda, salt, cinnamon and sugar. Make a well in center and stir in undrained raspberries and eggs. Thoroughly mix with oil and pecans. Spoon batter into lightly greased muffin tins. Cups will be full but batter is heavy and won't overflow. Bake 15 to 20 minutes. Cool 5 minutes before removing from pan. Yield: 1 dozen muffins.

♥ BLUEBERRY MUFFINS ♥

2 c. sifted flour
3 tsp. baking powder
1/3 c. sugar
3/4 tsp. salt

1 egg, beaten
3/4 c. milk
1/4 c. butter, melted
1 c. fresh blueberries

Sift flour, baking powder, sugar and salt together and add egg, milk and butter. Mix only until dry ingredients are moistened. Carefully fold in blueberries. Pour into greased muffin pans, filling pans 2/3 full. Bake at 425° for 20 to 25 minutes. Yield: 1 dozen muffins.

♥ BANANA BREAD ♥

1 3/4 c. all-purpose flour
2/3 c. sugar
2 tsp. baking powder
1/2 tsp. baking soda
1/4 tsp. salt
1 c. (2-3 medium) ripe bananas,
  mashed

1/3 c. shortening
2 T. milk
2 eggs
1/4 c. nuts, chopped

In a large bowl combine 1 cup flour, sugar, baking powder, baking soda and salt. Add mashed bananas, shortening and milk. Beat with an electric mixer on low speed until blended, then on high speed for 2 minutes. Add eggs and remaining flour; beat until blended. Stir in nuts. Pour batter into a greased 8 x 4 x 2-inch loaf pan. Bake in a 350° oven for 55 to 60 minutes or until a toothpick inserted near the center comes out clean. Cool for 10 minutes on a wire rack. Remove from pan; cool thoroughly on a wire rack. Wrap and store overnight before slicing. Yield: 1 loaf.

♥ QUICK TEA RING ♥

1/4 c. brown sugar
1 1/2 T. cream
1/4 c. butter
Nuts and/or cherries

1 tsp. cinnamon
1/2 c. sugar
2 (12-oz.) cans refrigerated biscuits
3 T. butter, melted

Mix brown sugar, cream, butter, nuts and cherries together in bowl. Place mixture in bottom of 1 1/2-quart salad mold. In small bowl mix cinnamon and sugar together. Dip each biscuit in remaining butter, then in cinnamon-sugar mixture. Place on top of nut mixture. Bake at 425° for 20 to 25 minutes. Yield: 6 to 8 servings.

♥ DANISH PUFF EASY ♥

2 c. flour, divided
1 c. + 2 T. butter
1 c. + 4 T. water

3 eggs
2½ tsp. vanilla or almond extract
1½ c. powdered sugar

Measure 1 cup flour into bowl and cut in ½ cup butter. Sprinkle 2 tablespoons water over mixture and mix with fork. Form into ball and divide in half. On ungreased cookie sheet, pat each half of dough with hands into 12 x 3-inch strips and place strips about 3 inches apart on cookie sheet. In a saucepan combine ½ cup butter and 1 cup water. Heat to boiling. Remove from heat and stir in 1 teaspoon vanilla extract. Beat in 1 cup flour, stirring to keep it from lumping. When smooth, add eggs one at a time, beating until smooth after each addition. Divide batter in half and spread each half evenly over strips already on cookie sheet. Bake at 350° for 1 hour or until topping is crisp and browned. Mix powdered sugar, 2 tablespoons butter, 1½ teaspoons vanilla extract and water until smooth. Frost glaze over cooled strips. Yield: 2 (6-serving) coffee cakes.

♥ LOVIN' SPOONFUL ROLLS ♥

1 pkg. dry yeast
2 c. warm water
¾ c. margarine, softened

¼ c. sugar
1 egg, beaten
4 c. self-rising flour

Place yeast in warm water. In separate dish cream softened margarine with sugar before adding egg. Add yeast water to creamed mixture, then add flour and stir until well mixed. To bake, drop by spoonfuls into well-greased 2½-inch muffin tins. Let rise until double in size. Bake at 350° about 20 minutes. This dough will keep for several days. To store, place in an airtight bowl and keep in refrigerator. Yield: 2 dozen rolls.

♥ ANGEL BISCUITS ♥

1 pkg. dry yeast
2 T. warm water
5 c. flour
¼ c. sugar
3 tsp. baking powder

1 tsp. soda
1 tsp. salt
1 c. shortening
3 c. buttermilk

Dissolve yeast in warm water. In separate bowl combine dry ingredients. Cut in shortening. Add yeast and buttermilk. Knead well until dough is smooth and elasticized. Roll out and cut with biscuit cutter. Bake at 375° for 15 to 20 minutes. Dough may be kept in covered dish in refrigerator until ready to use. Yield: 1 dozen biscuits.

♥ QUICK ROLLS ♥

2¼ c. baking mix, divided
1 (8-oz.) ctn. sour cream

½ c. butter, melted

Combine 2 cups baking mix, sour cream and butter, stirring well. Sprinkle remaining ¼ cup biscuit mix onto a flat surface. Drop dough by level tablespoon onto biscuit mix and roll into balls. Place 3 balls into each of 12 greased muffin cups. Bake at 375° for 15 minutes or until rolls are golden brown. Yield: 1 dozen rolls.

♥ CRAZY CORN BREAD ♥

2 eggs
1 c. milk
¼ c. oil
1 c. sifted flour
4 tsp. baking powder

1 tsp. salt
¼ c. sugar
1 c. yellow cornmeal
Butter (opt.)
Honey (opt.)

Beat eggs, milk and oil in bowl. In separate bowl sift together flour, baking powder, salt and sugar. Add flour mixture and cornmeal to egg mixture. Stir until batter is smooth. Pour mixture in greased 8 or 9-inch pan. Bake at 400° for 25 to 30 minutes. Serve with butter and honey as desired. Yield: 9 generous servings.

♥ HEART-SHAPED HERBED ROLLS ♥

1 (8-oz.) pkg. crescent rolls
1 tsp. Italian seasoning

1 T. margarine, softened

Cut rolls apart at the perforation. Spread all 8 triangles with margarine and sprinkle with Italian seasoning. Using a 2½-inch heart-shaped cutter, cut out hearts from each triangle. Place hearts on an ungreased baking sheet and bake at 375° for 11 to 13 minutes. Yield: 8 rolls.

"The meeting of two personalities is like the contact of two chemical substances: if there is any reaction, both are transformed."

--Carl Jung

♥ HERBED GARLIC BREAD ♥

½ c. butter, softened
1 clove garlic, minced
1 tsp. parsley flakes

¼ tsp. oregano
¼ tsp. dried dill, crushed
1 (1-lb.) loaf French bread

The flavor of this bread will be better if butter mixture is prepared several days before using. Combine butter, garlic, parsley, oregano and dill; refrigerate. Remove from refrigerator 1 hour before using to allow mixture to soften before spreading on bread. Cut bread into ¼-inch slices, not quite through bottom crust. Spread butter mixture generously between slices. Wrap loosely in foil. Heat on grill or in 350° oven for 15 minutes to toast. Yield: 8 to 10 servings.

♥ WINE, CHEESE & YOU BREAD ♥

1 c. + 2 T. all-purpose flour
½ tsp. baking powder
¼ tsp. cream of tartar
½ tsp. salt
⅛ tsp. baking soda
¼ c. instant nonfat dry milk
⅓ c. shortening

1 T. sugar
1 T. onion, minced
1 egg, beaten
¼ c. milk
¼ c. white wine
½ tsp. dried oregano
¼ c. Parmesan cheese, grated

Sift together flour, baking powder, cream of tartar, salt, soda and dry milk. Cut in shortening until the mixture resembles coarse meal. Add sugar, onion, egg, milk, wine and oregano. Mix thoroughly. Spread mixture in greased 8 or 9-inch round pan and sprinkle with cheese. Bake at 425° for 15 to 20 minutes or until toothpick inserted in center comes out clean. Yield: 8 servings.

♥ CHEESY BEER BREAD ♥

½ c. butter
3 c. self-rising flour
2 T. sugar
1 (12-oz.) can beer

¾ c. cheese, grated (opt.)
¼ c. jalapeños or chilies, chopped
(opt.)

Melt butter and pour enough to coat bottom of 9 x 5-inch loaf pan. In large bowl mix together flour, sugar and beer. Add cheese and jalapeños or chilies if desired. Mix well. Spoon dough into loaf pan. Pour remaining butter over top. Bake at 350° for 50 to 60 minutes or until bread is a light golden color. Let stand 10 minutes before cutting with a serrated knife. Yield: 8 servings.

♥ LITTLE LOVIN' BREAD STICKS ♥

1 (12-oz.) can refrigerated biscuits　　**1 c. Parmesan cheese, grated**
¼ c. butter

Cut each biscuit in half. Melt butter. Place Parmesan cheese in bowl. Dip each biscuit half in butter and then in the Parmesan cheese. Place biscuits on baking sheet and cook until brown according to biscuit instructions. Yield: 20 bread sticks.

♥ BEST BUDDIES CHEDDAR BREAD ♥

3⅓ c. baking mix　　　　　　　　**1¼ c. milk**
2 c. sharp Cheddar cheese,　　　　**2 eggs, slightly beaten**
**　shredded**

Preheat oven to 350°. Combine baking mix and cheese. Add milk and eggs, mixing just until moistened. Pour into greased and floured 9 x 5-inch loaf pan. Bake for 55 minutes before removing from pan. Serve warm. Yield: 8 servings.

♥ QUICK FIX FINGER ROLLS ♥

2 T. butter　　　　　　　　　　**Poppy seeds, sesame seeds,**
1 (7.5-oz.) pkg. refrigerated　　　**　Parmesan cheese, mixed herbs, or**
**　buttermilk biscuits**　　　　　　**　desired ingredients**

Melt butter in oven in a flat baking dish, like a pizza pan. Meanwhile, divide each of the 10 biscuits in half and roll into finger size. Roll into desired seasoning. When butter is melted, swirl it around so that bottom of pan is covered. Put rolls in pan with sides not touching. Bake 10 minutes at 400° or until golden brown. Yield: 10 servings.

"I get no kick from champagne.
Mere alcohol doesn't thrill me at all,
So tell me why should it be true
That I get a kick out of you."

--Cole Porter

♥ FOREVER FOCACCIA ♥

1¾ c. unbleached flour
1 (¼-oz.) pkg. dry yeast
1 tsp. sugar
¾ tsp. salt
¾ c. hot water (120-130°)
4-5½ T. olive oil
½ c. Gorgonzola cheese, crumbled

2 T. pine nuts
½ c. pesto (opt.)
½ c. feta cheese, crumbled (opt.)
6 sun-dried tomatoes, diced (opt.)
1 tsp. garlic, minced (opt.)
2 T. fresh or 1 T. dried rosemary
  (opt.)

In large bowl combine flour, yeast, sugar and salt. In small bowl combine water and 2½ tablespoons olive oil. Slowly add to flour mixture, stirring to form sticky dough. Turn dough out onto lightly floured surface, kneading in additional flour as needed until dough is smooth and elastic. Place dough in oiled bowl, turning to coat entire surface. Cover with plastic wrap or towel and let rise about 40 minutes or until dough is double in size. Preheat oven to 375°. Grease 13-inch round baking sheet. Punch dough down and let rest 5 minutes. Turn dough out onto lightly floured surface. Using floured rolling pin, roll dough into 12-inch round. Place on prepared baking sheet and build up edges of dough slightly to form crust. Cover as before and let rise 15 to 30 minutes. Pike indentations over surface of dough with fingers. Drizzle 2 tablespoons olive oil on dough and top with Gorgonzola cheese and pine nuts. Bake 30 minutes or until lightly browned on top and sides. Remove from oven and cool on baking sheet 5 minutes. Cut into wedges and serve warm. **Topping Options:** Instead of Gorgonzola and pine nuts, try topping the focaccia with a mixture of 1½ tablespoons olive oil, pesto, feta cheese and sun-dried tomatoes; or a mixture of 3 tablespoons olive oil, garlic and rosemary. Yield: 8 servings.

♥ PERFECT PIZZA DOUGH ♥

2½ c. flour
1 T. dry yeast
½ tsp. salt

1 c. warm water
1 T. oil
1 tsp. sugar or honey

Combine flour, yeast and salt in mixing bowl and stir. In separate bowl combine warm water, oil and sugar or honey and mix well. Add water mixture to dry ingredients and mix until well combined. Spread dough onto round pizza pan or rectangular cookie sheet and bake at 500° for 5 minutes. Turn over and cover with pizza sauce and toppings. Bake another 15 minutes at 425°. Yield: 1 (14-inch) crust.

♥ WHOLE WHEAT PIZZA DOUGH ♥

1 c. warm water
1 pkg. active dry yeast or ¼ oz.
  compressed yeast
1½ c. unbleached all-purpose flour

1 c. whole-wheat flour
2 T. olive oil
½ tsp. salt

Combine water, yeast and all-purpose flour in a large bowl. Mix well. Add whole-wheat flour, oil and salt. You may need a bit less flour so add the whole-wheat flour gradually. With your hands or a large wooden spoon, work ingredients together until dough holds its shape. Place dough on a lightly floured surface and knead for 5 minutes or until smooth and elastic. If dough becomes sticky while kneading it, sprinkle a bit more all-purpose flour over it. Transfer dough to a lightly oiled 2-quart bowl. Cover bowl with plastic wrap or a kitchen towel and let rise for 1 hour or until it has doubled in size. When dough has risen, place it on a lightly floured surface, divide it into two or more parts and roll them into balls. Cover them with a towel and let them rise for 15 to 20 minutes. The dough can now be shaped, put on pizza pans, topped and cooked. Yield: 2 (12-inch) crusts - 4 servings; 4 (6-inch) - 4 servings; or 8 (3-inch) - appetizer portions.

Through thee alone the sky is arched,
Through thee the rose is red;
All things through thee take nobler form,
And look beyond the earth,
The mill-round of our fate appears
A sun-path in thy worth.
Me too thy nobleness has taught
To master my despair;
The fountains of my hidden life
Are through thy friendship fair.

--Ralph Waldo Emerson

Our Favorite Recipes

HOT, HOT HOT!

Soups
& Stews

From Shower to Showcase

Tips for keeping your
wedding gifts beautiful

Once the big day is over and the gifts have all been unwrapped, some lucky brides will own their first sets of china, crystal and silver. Even though many of these items will be packed lovingly into cabinets, hutches or curios to be brought out for special occasions, you'll want to keep them looking like they did on your wedding day. With a little care and the following tips, you may be able to keep them around for years.

A good set of silverware should occasionally be shined with silver polish using long strokes, never a circular motion. Avoid especially gritty polishes and be careful not to polish too hard. Remember, some darker areas may seem like flaws but are really part of the design. Another way to keep silverware clean is to store it in specially treated silver cloth, which absorbs tarnish-producing gases before they reach the silver.

When it's time to store silver, remember silver reacts chemically to acidic materials. If you're wrapping utensils, use acid-free wrappings instead of acidic ones like newspapers. Also, don't store silver in oak cabinets or shelves, as oak also contains acidic substances.

China and porcelain dishes scratch and mar easily and must be handled with extra care. Avoid drastic temperature changes with these dishes. Many also have a gold or silver lining or rim, which can scratch during cleaning. To shine up items rinse them in a sinkful of warm water mixed with 1/2 cup borax, and rinse again with clear water.

If you aren't displaying china in a cabinet, separate the dishes with cloth napkins to keep them from chipping. Don't stack cups inside one another as the coloring could rub off or the handles could break.

Though not as sensitive, crystal still requires a gentle touch. Much of today's crystal can stand the heat of a dishwasher. If you don't trust a machine, line the sink with plastic, rubber or even a towel to avoid shipping the glass as you wash.

Sometimes a film builds up on cut glassware. If this happens, wash your glassware decanters in a solution of one part vinegar to three parts water. Particularly dirty decanters can be cleaned by filling them with warm water, 1 tablespoon baking powder and some crushed eggshells. Leave the solution in the decanter for 12 hours and rinse with warm water.

Glass should be dried with a lint free towel or polished by rubbing with tissue paper. When storing crystal, consider covering the shelves with felt or thick paper to prevent chipping. Before getting rid of a chipped piece, remember that some small nicks can be smoothed away with emery paper.

Hot, Hot, Hot!

♥ JUST LIKE MOM'S CHICKEN ♥ NOODLE SOUP

1 whole chicken or stewing hen
2 onions, halved
4 whole cloves
3 qts. water
4 stalks celery, with leaves
4 carrots, peeled
3 parsnips, peeled (opt.)
3 cloves garlic
6 sprigs fresh or 1 tsp. dried dill

6 sprigs parsley
Salt and pepper to taste
1 cube chicken bouillon
Noodles
1½ c. peas, cooked or frozen
¼ c. fresh dill, chopped
2 T. fresh or 1 T. dried parsley, chopped

Rinse chicken well and place in large soup pot. Stud each onion half with a clove and add to pot along with water, celery, carrots, parsnips, garlic, dill, parsley, salt and pepper. Simmer for 2 hours and occasionally skim off any foam that forms on top. Remove chicken from soup and allow to cool. Remove skin and bones and shred meat. Reserve meat, covered, in refrigerator. Strain soup and discard vegetables. Return liquid to pot and add bouillon cube and more seasonings if desired. Bring to a boil and cook, uncovered for 10 minutes. Before serving bring chicken broth to gentle boil. Add homemade or pre-made noodles and cook until they are tender. Gently stir in reserved chicken and peas, dill and parsley. Heat through and serve. Yield: 8 servings.

♥ EASY CHICKEN NOODLE SOUP ♥

7-8 c. water
2 cans chicken or 2 c. chicken, cooked and cubed
2 tsp. onion, minced

1½ tsp. parsley flakes
6 T. chicken bouillon granules
1 (12-oz.) pkg. frozen egg noodles

In large saucepan bring water, chicken, onion and 1¼ teaspoon parsley flakes to a boil. Add bouillon granules and dissolve. Drop in frozen noodles and stir to separate. Simmer 50 minutes. For color, sprinkle in ¼ teaspoon parsley flakes just before serving. Yield: 4 servings.

♥ MINESTRONE MAMA MIA! ♥

5-6 oz. salt pork, thinly sliced
1 yellow onion, thinly sliced
1 leek, thinly sliced
2 carrots, pared and thinly sliced
2 potatoes, pared and thinly sliced
1 c. tomatoes, thinly sliced
¼ celery root, peeled and diced
2 T. tomato paste

Pepper to taste
2 cloves garlic
2 qts. chicken stock
1 c. broken spaghetti
1½ tsp. basil
Parsley, chopped, to taste
Salt (opt.)
Parmesan cheese, grated, to taste

Cut salt pork and all vegetables into thin strips about 2 inches long. Sauté the pork without allowing it to brown. Add tomato paste and season with pepper. Press juice from garlic cloves into pork mixture. Add sliced onion, leek, carrots, potatoes, tomatoes and celery. Pour in chicken stock and let soup boil, uncovered, for 10 minutes. Add spaghetti and season with basil and parsley. Add salt only if needed. Cook until spaghetti is al dente. Sprinkle with Parmesan cheese before serving. Yield: 6 to 8 servings.

♥ MINESTRONE SOUP ♥

1 lb. ground beef
Garlic to taste
7-8 c. water
8 tsp. chicken bouillon granules
2 T. dry celery flakes
2 T. dry minced onion
1 tsp. Italian seasoning
1-2 tsp. Italian dressing mix

1 c. ketchup
1 (15-oz.) can kidney beans, drained
1 (1-lb.) pkg. frozen Italian vegetables, drained
1 c. macaroni
Parmesan cheese, grated (opt.)

Brown ground beef with desired amount of garlic. Drain beef and remove any excess fat from pan. Add all remaining ingredients and simmer for 30 minutes. Serve with Parmesan cheese as desired. Yield: 6 (2-cup) servings.

♥ BEEF VEGETABLE SOUP ♥

1 lb. ground beef
1 (16-oz.) pkg. frozen mixed vegetables

2 c. beef bouillon broth
2 c. potatoes, chopped
Salt and pepper to taste

Brown ground beef in saucepan, stirring until crumbly; drain. Stir in remaining ingredients. Simmer for 30 minutes before serving. Yield: 4 servings.

♥ HEART AND HOME SOUP ♥

1 chuck roast
Water
2 tsp. salt
1 (28-oz.) can crushed tomatoes
1 onion, chopped
¾ c. celery
1 (16-oz.) pkg. frozen mixed
  vegetables

1 sm. head cabbage, shredded
1 tsp. sugar
Salt and pepper to taste
5 beef bouillon cubes
2 carrots, sliced
2 potatoes, cubed

The night before you plan to serve dish, cook the roast in enough water to cover and 2 teaspoons salt until roast is tender. When done, cut roast into small pieces and throw away all fat and bones. Put meat in covered bowl and refrigerate. Put the broth in a separate bowl and refrigerate overnight. The next day skim fat off top of dish and discard. Heat remaining broth and add all other ingredients, including meat. Simmer for 1½ to 2 hours on low heat. Yield: 6 to 8 servings.

♥ RED HOT TOMATO SOUP ♥

1 stalk celery, chopped
¼ c. onion, chopped
2 tsp. margarine
1 T. lemon juice

1 tsp. sugar
1 (10½-oz.) can tomato soup
1 soup can water
1 T. parsley

Sauté celery and onion in margarine until tender and crisp. Add other ingredients and heat until serving time. Yield: 2 servings.

"Give me a kiss, and to that kiss a score;
Then to that twenty, add a hundred more;
A thousand to that hundred: so kiss on,
To make that thousand up a million.
Treble that million, and when that is done,
Let's kiss afresh, as when we first begun."
--Robert Herrick

♥ VEGGIE CHILI ♥

½ c. olive oil
2 zucchini, cut into ½-inch cubes
2 onions, cut into ½-inch cubes
4 cloves garlic, finely chopped
2 lg. red bell peppers, cored and
cut into ¼-inch cubes
1 (35-oz.) can Italian plum
tomatoes, with juice
1½ lbs. ripe plum tomatoes, cut
into 1-inch cubes
2 T. chili powder
1 T. ground cumin
1 T. dried basil

1 T. dried oregano
2 tsp. pepper
1 tsp. salt
1 tsp. fennel seeds
½ c. fresh parsley, chopped
1 c. canned dark red kidney beans,
drained
1 c. canned chickpeas, drained
½ c. fresh dill, chopped
2 T. lemon juice
1 c. sour cream
2 c. Monterey Jack cheese, grated
4 scallions, sliced diagonally

Heat ¼ cup of oil in large skillet over medium heat. Add zucchini and sauté
5 to 7 minutes or until just tender. Transfer zucchini to large flameproof
casserole dish or Dutch oven. Heat remaining ¼ cup oil in skillet over low
heat. Add onions, garlic and bell peppers. Sauté 10 minutes or until just wilted.
Transfer mixture to casserole dish. Place dish over low heat. Add tomatoes,
chili powder, cumin, basil, oregano, pepper, salt, fennel seeds and parsley.
Cook, uncovered, for 30 minutes, stirring often. Stir in kidney beans, chickpeas,
dill and lemon juice. Cook for another 15 minutes. Stir and adjust seasonings
to taste. Garnish and serve with sour cream, cheese and scallions. Yield:
8 servings.

♥ CHILI FOR LOVERS ♥

2-3 lbs. ground beef or turkey
1 lg. onion, chopped
1 lg. green pepper, chopped
3 (15-oz.) cans kidney beans
2 (14-oz.) cans tomatoes

6 whole cloves
2 bay leaves
2-3 T. chili powder
Dash cayenne pepper
Dash paprika

Sauté ground meat with onions and peppers until meat is browned and crumbly.
Add beans, tomatoes, cloves, bay leaves, chili powder, cayenne and paprika.
Simmer 2 to 3 hours. Remove bay leaves before serving. Yield: 6 servings.

*"A successful marriage requires falling in love many
times, always with the same person."*

--Mignon McLaughlin

♥ PLEASIN' POTATO SOUP ♥

4 c. potatoes, cut in 1-inch cubes
2 med. onions, sliced
³/₄ c. water
1 tsp. salt
¹/₂ tsp. garlic salt

¹/₂ tsp. oregano
¹/₄ tsp. pepper
3 c. milk
¹/₄ c. butter

Combine first 7 ingredients in large pan. Cover and bring to a boil, then simmer for about 20 minutes until potatoes are tender. Mash potatoes slightly. Add milk and butter. Heat through. Yield: 4 servings.

♥ BROCCOLI CHEESE SOUP ♥

1 (10-oz.) pkg. chopped broccoli
1 (10¹/₂-oz.) can Cheddar cheese soup

1 soup can milk
1 c. Cheddar cheese, shredded

Cook broccoli as directed on package. Heat Cheddar cheese soup, milk and shredded Cheddar cheese together. Add cooked broccoli and mix well. Yield: 2 servings.

♥ SATISFYING BEAN SOUP ♥

2 c. dried beans
Water
2 T. salt
1 ham hock or smoked turkey
1 lg. onion

1 qt. tomato juice
1 tsp. chili powder
3 T. lemon juice
¹/₂ tsp. basil
Salt and pepper

Wash beans and cover with water in large kettle. Add salt and soak overnight. Drain. Add water and ham hock or turkey and heat. Bring to a boil and simmer slowly for 2 hours. Add onion, tomato juice, chili powder, lemon juice, basil, salt and pepper. Remove meat. Cut up and return to soup. Simmer for 1 hour before serving. Yield: 4 servings.

♥ SPLIT PEA SOUP ♥

1 lb. split peas
2 c. water
1 (47-oz.) can chicken broth
3 slices bacon, chopped
¹/₂ tsp. dry mustard

1 c. celery, diced
¹/₄ tsp. pepper
1 tsp. salt
¹/₈ tsp. oregano
1 c. ham, diced

In a large pot combine all ingredients except oregano and ham. Cover and simmer 3 to 4 hours. Skim off any fat. Add oregano and ham and simmer 1 hour. Serve hot. Yield: 6 servings.

♥ OOH LA LA FRENCH ONION SOUP ♥

4 lg. onions, sliced thin
1/4 c. butter
1 T. flour
6 beef bouillon cubes

4 c. water
1 tsp. Worcestershire sauce
Bread slices
1/3 c. Parmesan cheese, grated

Sauté onion in butter until golden. Stir in flour. Add bouillon, water and Worcestershire sauce. Simmer for 20 minutes, stirring occasionally. Serve topped with toasted bread slices and sprinkled with Parmesan cheese. Yield: 4 servings.

♥ WONTON LOVE SOUP ♥

1/2 lb. ground pork
1 egg
1 T. onion, grated
4 tsp. salt

2 T. soy sauce
Wonton wrappers
6 c. chicken broth

Brown ground pork. Combine with egg, onion, 2 teaspoons salt and 1 tablespoon soy sauce. Wrap small amount of meat mixture in wonton wrappers, fold in triangle and wet edges with water to make them stick together. Combine chicken broth, 1 tablespoon soy sauce and 2 teaspoons salt. Add filled wontons and simmer until heated through. Yield: 4 servings.

♥ HOT AND SOUR SOUP ♥

3 (10 1/2-oz.) cans chicken broth
1/2 lb. mushrooms, thinly sliced
1/2 lb. boneless pork, cut into thin
  strips
1/2 c. bamboo shoots
5 T. distilled vinegar
3 T. soy sauce
1/2 tsp. red pepper flakes

1/4 tsp. pepper
1/4 lb. tofu, cubed
1/4 c. cold water
3 T. cornstarch
1 egg, beaten
2 tsp. sesame oil
1/4 c. green onions

In a 3-quart pan bring chicken broth to a boil. Add mushrooms, pork, bamboo shoots, vinegar, soy sauce, red pepper flakes and pepper. Cover and simmer 5 minutes. Add tofu and bring to a boil. In cold water dissolve cornstarch. Stir in 1/2 cup hot soup. Add mixture to soup and cook, stirring, for 2 minutes. Slowly add egg to hot soup. Stir gently once or twice. Sprinkle with sesame oil and green onions. Yield: 4 to 6 servings.

♥ HEARTY MAN SOUP ♥

1 lb. lean ground chuck
5 c. water or beef broth
1 (14-oz.) can stewed tomatoes
1 (6-oz.) can vegetable juice
1/3 c. pearl barley
1/3 c. dried split green peas
1/2 c. onion, chopped

1 T. beef bouillon granules
1/4 tsp. pepper
1/4 tsp. dried basil
1/4 tsp. dried oregano
1 bay leaf
3/4 c. celery with leaves, chopped
1/2 c. carrots, diced

Spray bottom of kettle with cooking spray. Brown meat, stirring to crumble. Drain off any oil. Add water or broth, tomatoes, vegetable juice, barley, peas, onion, bouillon, pepper, basil, oregano and bay leaf. Bring to a boil and reduce heat to simmer for 30 minutes. Add celery and carrots. Bring to a boil and simmer another 30 minutes. Remove bay leaf before serving. Yield: 6 servings.

♥ SO GREAT SANTA FE SOUP ♥

2 chicken breasts, cooked, skinned
   and cut into small pieces
1 (46-oz.) can tomato juice
1 (16-oz.) jar picante sauce

2 c. cooked rice
1 c. Cheddar or American cheese,
   grated
1 c. tortilla chips, crushed

In a large pot combine chicken, tomato juice, picante sauce and rice. Heat thoroughly. Serve topped with cheese and chips. Yield: 8 servings.

♥ COMFY CORN CHOWDER ♥

8 slices bacon
1 lg. onion, chopped
2 c. water
3 c. milk

2 c. cream-style corn
2 tsp. salt
Pepper to taste
4 potatoes, pared and diced

Fry bacon until crisp. Drain on paper towel and break into pieces. Sauté onion in a large pot in 2 tablespoons bacon grease. Add water, milk, corn, salt, pepper and potatoes. Cook until potatoes are done and then simmer for 1 hour. Sprinkle with bacon pieces and serve. Yield: 8 to 9 cups.

"Variety is the soul of pleasure."

--Aphra Behn

♥ CRAZY CLAM CHOWDER ♥

1 c. onion, finely chopped
1 c. celery, finely chopped
2 c. potatoes, diced
2 (10-oz.) cans minced clams with
  juice
Water

³/₄ c. butter
³/₄ c. flour
1 qt. half-and-half
1¹/₂ tsp. salt
Pepper to taste
2 T. wine vinegar

In saucepan cover onions, celery, potatoes and clams with clam juice and water. Simmer mixture until vegetables are tender. In another pan, melt butter and whisk in flour. Add half-and-half and whisk. Add undrained vegetables, clams, salt, pepper and vinegar. Heat slowly. Yield: 6 to 8 servings.

♥ BEEF STEW ♥

¹/₂ c. vegetable oil
1-1¹/₂ lbs. beef, cubed
Salt and pepper to taste
1 onion, chopped
1 (16-oz.) can cream of mushroom
  soup
¹/₂ soup can milk

3 c. water
Carrots, chopped
Potatoes, chopped
Green beans or frozen stew
  vegetables
Turnips, chopped

Turn crockpot on low. Add oil, meat, salt, pepper and onions. Let simmer for about 3 hours. Add cream of mushroom soup, milk, water and vegetables. Turn crockpot on high and stir off and on throughout the day. Cook until vegetables are tender. Yield: 6 to 8 servings.

"Marriage resembles a pair of shears, so joined that they cannot be separated, often moving in opposite directions, yet always punishing anyone who comes between them."
--Sydney Smith

BRIDE-06

GETTING FRESH

Salads

Loving Where You Live

Ideas for decorating your dining area at minimal cost

Sprucing up your first dining area or holding your first post-wedding party can be intimidating for any novice hostess. Fear not, creative catering doesn't have to be difficult or costly. With minimal skill, time and money you can prepare a party your peers will chat about for weeks.

If you're short on decorations, be inventive and take advantage of all mother nature has to offer. Add a creative twist to centerpieces, napkin rings and candlesticks by using autumn leaves painted gold and silver, or threading chains of daisies and other lawn flora. Dig through drawers for items that will add character to your table, like cookie cutters used as napkin rings. They're cheap, reusable and can easily adapt to your party theme.

A second-hand mirror makes an elegant centerpiece when covered with candles. Candlelight is not only romantic, it also disguises flaws that jump out during the day. That big basket Aunt Agatha filled with towels for your bridal shower can be refilled with fragrant flowers or a selection of pine cones and evergreen sprays. And Aunt Agatha will be pleased you're still using her gift.

Take an assortment of old mayonnaise jars, unused vases and colored glass liquor bottles and add a little paint, ribbon, glitter and elbow grease. You now have some innovative and beautiful containers for holding breadsticks, flatware, wine bottles, condiments, or anything your heart desires.

Terra cotta flower pots, sans potting soil of course, make unique containers for baked bread or pot pie. Pumpkin or squash shells are fun soup servers after their contents have been scooped out, while seeded and cored peppers can hold a spicy dip.

Can't stand the site of your scratched hand-me-down table? Can't believe the prices of new damask table cloths? Make your own table coverings without picking up a needle and thread. Just take a bed sheet or a ruffly curtain, throw on a brightly-colored scarf and you'll set the scene for a perfect meal.

Not every occasion will be a formal affair, but sometimes you and your dining room will have to slip on the black tie. If you don't know which spoon goes where, follow the simple diagram to the left, omitting whatever you don't need or don't have.

Getting Fresh

♥ LETTUCE BE TOGETHER SALAD ♥

1 head lettuce, chopped
½ head cauliflower, chopped
1 onion, chopped fine
Cheddar cheese, shredded
8 strips bacon, fried and crumbled

1 c. mayonnaise or salad dressing
2 T. mustard
2 tsp. vinegar
½ c. sugar
Salt to taste

Toss together lettuce, cauliflower, onion, cheese and bacon. In a separate bowl make dressing by mixing together mayonnaise or salad dressing, mustard, vinegar, sugar and salt. Just before serving add to lettuce mixture and toss. Serve immediately. Yield: 6 servings.

♥ CAESAR SALAD ♥

2 heads romaine lettuce
¾ c. Parmesan cheese, grated
1 c. croutons
¼ c. lemon juice
¼ c. red wine vinegar
¾ c. olive oil
1 lg. anchovy fillet (opt.)

1-3 lg. garlic cloves, pressed or
 minced fine
Pepper to taste
Dash Worcestershire sauce
1 egg, coddled 3 minutes in boiling
 water

Wash, dry and tear lettuce into bite-size pieces. Place lettuce, cheese and croutons in a large salad bowl. In a small bowl blend together lemon juice, vinegar and oil; set aside. In another small bowl mash anchovy to a paste; add garlic, pepper and Worcestershire sauce. Add egg and mix well. Beat in lemon juice mixture until thoroughly blended. Pour desired amount of dressing over salad greens, a little at a time. Toss and serve. Yield: 8 to 10 servings.

♥ SPECIAL SPINACH SALAD ♥

1½ c. fresh spinach leaves, washed
  and torn
5 med. fresh mushrooms, sliced
1 hard-cooked egg, chopped
1 onion, sliced and separated into
  rings

1 tsp. bacon bits
2 tsp. vegetable oil
1½ tsp. red wine vinegar
¼ tsp. dry mustard
1 tsp. water

Place spinach on a salad plate. Top with mushrooms, egg, onion and bacon bits. In a small bowl combine oil, vinegar, mustard and water. Pour over salad, toss and serve. Yield: 2 servings.

♥ SWEETIE'S SPINACH SALAD ♥

1½ lbs. fresh spinach
2 oranges
½ red onion
3-4 green onions
2 T. brown sugar

¼ c. cider vinegar
½ tsp. dry mustard
½ tsp. celery seed
½ tsp. paprika
½ c. canola or olive oil

Wash spinach thoroughly and remove stems. Tear into bite sized pieces and place in a large serving bowl; chill. Peel oranges and cut into segments, reserving the juice. Cut onions into thin slices and soak in ice water for 10 minutes. Add oranges and drained onion slices to spinach. In a small bowl mix together sugar, vinegar, mustard, celery seed, paprika and fruit juices. Gradually whisk in oil. Pour half of dressing over salad, adding more if needed, and serve. Yield: 6 to 8 servings.

♥ LAYERED WITH LOVE SALAD ♥

1 head lettuce, shredded
1 (8-oz.) can water chestnuts
1 (16-oz.) pkg. frozen peas
1 lg. onion, sliced

½ c. bacon bits or crumbled bacon
1 c. mayonnaise
1 c. sour cream
Parmesan cheese, grated

The day before you plan to serve this dish, layer lettuce, water chestnuts, peas, onion and bacon in a 9 x 13-inch dish or truffle bowl. Seal top layer with a mixture of mayonnaise and sour cream. Top with Parmesan cheese and refrigerate overnight. Yield: 8 to 10 servings.

♥ MARINATED BEAN SALAD ♥

2 (8-oz.) cans green beans, drained
1 (8-oz.) can pitted black olives, drained
1 (4-oz.) can pimentos, drained and chopped (opt.)
1 (4-oz.) can sliced mushrooms, drained
1 c. Italian dressing

Combine beans, olives, pimentos and mushrooms in a large bowl. Pour Italian dressing over mixture. Let mixture marinate overnight in refrigerator before serving. Yield: 4 to 6 servings.

♥ MACARONI SALAD ♥

3 c. assorted fresh vegetables, chopped
2 oz. broad egg noodles or macaroni, cooked and drained
1/4 c. creamy Italian dressing

In medium bowl combine vegetables and noodles. Toss with Italian dressing to coat well. Cover and refrigerate salad until ready to serve. Yield: 4 servings.

♥ TWO PEAS IN A POD SALAD ♥

1 (10-oz.) pkg. frozen peas, thawed
1 c. celery, finely chopped
1 c. cauliflower, finely chopped
1/2 c. sunflower seeds
1/2 c. sour cream
1 c. Ranch dressing

In large bowl combine all ingredients together. Chill before serving. Yield: 4 servings.

♥ ITALIAN SALAD ♥

3/4 lb. mozzarella cheese, sliced into 1/4-inch thick rounds
2-3 ripe tomatoes, cut into 1/4-inch thick slices
Extra virgin olive oil to taste
1 T. fresh basil, chopped
Salt and pepper to taste

On a large serving platter arrange rows or rings of alternating and slightly overlapping slices of mozzarella cheese and tomatoes. Drizzle a thin line of olive oil down the center of each row of slices. Do not add spices if preparing dish ahead of time. Cover and store dish in the refrigerator until time of use. Before serving, allow dish to warm to room temperature and add basil, salt and pepper to taste. Yield: 4 servings.

♥ CORN AND BARLEY SALAD ♥

2 c. water
1 c. barley
3 T. olive oil
2 T. lime juice
1 clove garlic, minced
¼ tsp. salt
Pepper to taste

½ c. red onion, chopped
2-3 green onions, thinly sliced
1 green or red bell pepper, cored,
  seeded and diced
1 c. corn, cooked
¼ c. fresh cilantro, chopped

Bring water to a boil. Add barley to water, cover and simmer for 50 to 60 minutes or until barley is tender. While barley is cooking, whisk together a dressing of olive oil, lime juice, garlic, salt and pepper in a separate bowl. Once barley is cooked, add the dressing mixture to it. Add remaining ingredients and mix well. Serve immediately. Yield: 6 to 8 servings.

♥ BROWN RICE SALAD ♥

1 c. raw brown rice
2½ c. chicken broth, defatted
2 tsp. dried marjoram
¼ tsp. salt
1 avocado, peeled, pitted and diced
½ c. fresh parsley, minced

½ c. green or red onion, chopped
1 tomato, cored and chopped
5 T. lemon juice
3 T. olive oil
Pepper to taste

In a saucepan combine rice, chicken broth, marjoram and salt. Bring mixture to a boil. Reduce heat, cover and simmer for 40 to 45 minutes; cool. In a medium bowl combine avocado, parsley, onion, tomato, lemon juice and olive oil. Season to taste with pepper. Gently combine avocado mixture with rice mixture and serve. This makes a meal! Yield: 6 to 8 servings.

"How delightful is your love, my sister, my bride! How much more pleasing is your love than wine, and the fragrance of your perfume than any spice!"
--Song of Solomon 4:10

♥ GREEN BEANS NICOISE ♥

1½ lbs. fresh green beans, cut into
  2-inch pieces
2 red potatoes, cooked and cubed
  but not peeled
½ c. sliced black olives, rinsed and
  drained
¼ c. walnuts, chopped
2 tomatoes, cored and wedged

½ c. onion, chopped
½ c. plain yogurt
1 T. olive oil
3 T. fresh dill, chopped or 1 T.
  dried dill
1 tsp. lemon juice
¼ tsp. salt
¼ tsp. white pepper

Steam green beans until tender-crisp and cool. In a large bowl toss together beans, potatoes, olives, nuts, tomatoes and onions. In a small bowl whisk together yogurt, olive oil, dill, lemon juice, salt and pepper. Pour yogurt mixture over green bean mixture and toss together well. Serve chilled or at room temperature. Yield: 6 to 8 servings.

♥ SLAW FOR TWO ♥

1 c. cabbage, shredded
¼ c. carrot, shredded
¼ c. celery, chopped
¼ c. green pepper, chopped
2 T. vegetable oil

2 T. mayonnaise
1 tsp. prepared mustard
¼ tsp. hot pepper sauce
Salt to taste

In a medium bowl combine cabbage, carrot, celery and green pepper. In another bowl combine oil, mayonnaise, mustard, hot pepper sauce and salt. Pour oil mixture over vegetables and toss together. Cover and chill for several hours. Stir slaw before serving. Yield: 2 servings.

♥ POTATO SALAD L'AMOUR ♥

1½ tsp. salt
1 c. water
2 lbs. (6 med.) potatoes
1 sm. (¼ c.) onion, finely chopped
¼ c. Italian dressing

⅛ tsp. pepper
½ c. mayonnaise
1 med. (¼ c.) stalk celery, chopped
2 hard-boiled eggs, coarsely
  chopped

Add ½ teaspoon salt to water and heat to boiling. Add potatoes and reduce heat. Cover and cook for about 30 to 35 minutes or until potatoes are tender; drain and cool. Cut potatoes into cubes. Stir in onion, Italian dressing, remaining salt and pepper. Cover and refrigerate mixture for at least two hours. Just before serving mix in mayonnaise until potatoes are well coated. Add celery and eggs and mix. Yield: 4 to 6 servings.

♥ CREAMY AND DREAMY CUCUMBERS ♥

½ c. sour cream or plain yogurt
1 T. vinegar or lemon juice
1 tsp. sugar
¼ tsp. dried dill weed (opt.)
1 tsp. salt

Dash pepper
1 lg. (3 c.) cucumber, halved
lengthwise and thinly sliced
1 sm. onion, thinly sliced and
separated into rings

In a large bowl stir together sour cream, vinegar, sugar, dill weed, salt and pepper. Add cucumber and onion rings. Toss to coat. Cover and chill mixture for 2 to 48 hours, stirring often, before serving. Yield: 6 side dish servings.

♥ ELEGANT CRAB LOUIS ♥

1 med. head iceberg lettuce
2 (6-oz.) pkgs. frozen crabmeat,
thawed, or 2 (7-oz.) cans
crabmeat, chilled, drained and
cartilage removed
2 lg. tomatoes, wedged
2 hard-boiled eggs, wedged
½ c. mayonnaise or salad dressing
¼ c. green pepper, finely chopped

¼ c. green onion, finely chopped
2 T. chili sauce
1 T. milk
½ tsp. lemon juice
Dash Worcestershire sauce
¼ c. whipping cream
Paprika
1 lemon, wedged

Remove 4 large leaves from lettuce head and place one each on 4 salad plates before setting aside. Tear remaining lettuce into bite-size pieces and top lettuce leaves. Reserve 4 large pieces of crabmeat and set aside. Flake remaining crabmeat and arrange it, tomatoes and eggs on lettuce beds. In a bowl mix mayonnaise, green pepper, onion, chili sauce, milk, lemon juice and Worcestershire sauce. In a separate bowl beat whipping cream into soft peaks. Fold whipped cream into mayonnaise mixture. Drizzle dressing mixture over arrangements. Sprinkle with paprika and garnish with reserved crabmeat and lemon wedges. Yield: 4 main dish servings.

♥ PICNIC PAIRS CHICKEN SALAD ♥

1-2 c. chicken, cooked and chopped
1 c. carrots, grated
1 c. celery, diced
1 c. frozen peas

1 c. mayonnaise or salad dressing
1 (20-oz.) pkg. shoestring potatoes
1 (2-oz.) pkg. almonds

Mix chicken, carrots, celery and peas together in a bowl. Mix in mayonnaise and chill mixture for 24 hours. Before serving, add cooked shoestring potatoes and almonds and mix well. Yield: 4 to 6 servings.

♥ TEX-MEX CHICKEN SALAD ♥

1 pkg. frozen chicken breast
  tenders
4 c. lettuce, shredded
1 (15-oz.) can chili hot beans,
  drained and liquid reserved
1 c. tomato, chopped

1 c. Cheddar cheese, shredded
¼ c. chunky salsa
2 c. tortilla chips
Sour cream

Prepare chicken as package directs and set aside. In a bowl combine lettuce, drained beans, tomato and cheese and top with chicken. In a separate bowl combine salsa and reserved chili bean liquid. Pour over chicken and lettuce mixture. Serve with chips and sour cream. Yield: 4 servings.

♥ LOVEABLE LIME GREEN SALAD ♥

1 c. vegetable or olive oil
⅓ c. lime juice
3 T. sugar
1½ tsp. salt
⅛ tsp. white pepper
⅛ tsp. cayenne pepper
¼ tsp. celery salt

6 paper-thin slices lime
1½ qts. mixed salad greens
½ c. black olives, sliced (opt.)
Artichoke hearts, sliced (opt.)
Red or yellow pepper, cut into
  strips (opt.)

In a bowl mix together oil, lime juice, sugar, salt, white pepper, cayenne pepper and celery salt. Shake or beat mixture until well blended. Just before serving, add lime slices to salad greens. Shake dressing again and pour over salad greens, using just enough dressing to coat the leaves well. Toss lightly and serve, garnished with choice of olives, artichoke slices or pepper strips. Yield: 8 servings.

♥ RASPBERRY VALENTINE SALAD ♥

2 T. raspberry vinegar
2 T. raspberry jam
⅓ c. vegetable oil
8 c. fresh spinach, rinsed, stemmed
  and torn into bite-size pieces

¾ c. macadamia nuts or pecans,
  chopped
1 c. fresh raspberries
3 kiwis, peeled and sliced

To prepare dressing, combine vinegar and jam in blender or food processor and mix. Add oil in a thin stream, blending well, and set aside. In a large bowl toss spinach, ½ of the nuts, ½ of the raspberries and ½ of the kiwis with the dressing. Put individual servings on salad plates or in shallow bowls. Top mixture with remaining nuts, raspberries and kiwis. Serve immediately. This recipe may also be substituted with strawberry vinegar, strawberry jam and fresh strawberries. Yield: 6 to 8 servings.

♥ SWEET ORANGE CARROT SALAD ♥

3 c. carrots, shredded
3 T. lemon juice
1/2 tsp. ground cinnamon

2 (11-oz.) cans mandarin oranges,
  drained
1 T. sugar

Place carrots in a medium bowl. Add remaining ingredients and toss well. Cover and chill for several hours before serving. Yield: 6 servings.

♥ GRANDMA'S CARROT SALAD ♥

1 lb. carrots, shredded
1/2 c. sour cream

1/4 c. sugar
1 c. raisins

Place shredded carrots in mixing bowl. In separate bowl mix sour cream and sugar together and then pour over carrots. Add raisins and toss together until all ingredients are evenly distributed and moist. Put mixture in a plastic container and cover with a tight lid. Refrigerate until ready to serve. Yield: 6 to 8 servings.

♥ CITRUS MIXED SALAD ♥

1 pink or red grapefruit
1 blood or navel orange
1/4 c. salad oil
1/2 tsp. lemon peel, finely shredded
2 T. lemon juice
1 tsp. sugar

2 tsp. Dijon mustard
1/4 tsp. pepper
2 c. Belgian endive, thinly sliced
2 c. escarole, torn
1/2 sm. (1 c.) jicama, peeled and cut
  into matchsticks

Over a large bowl peel and section grapefruit and orange, reserving any juices. Cover and set aside or chill until needed. In a lidded container combine grapefruit and orange juices, oil, lemon peel, lemon juice, sugar, mustard and pepper. Cover and shake well. On individual salad plates place Belgian endive and escarole. Arrange grapefruit, orange and jicama on top of the greens. Drizzle dressing over each serving and serve immediately. Yield: 4 to 6 servings.

♥ WALDORF SALAD ♥

1 lg. apple, diced but unpeeled
1 T. lemon juice
1/2 c. celery, chopped

3 lg. walnuts, coarsely crushed
10 seedless grapes, halved
2 1/2 T. yogurt with fruit

In a bowl sprinkle diced apples with lemon juice. Add celery, nuts and grapes and mix well. Combine mixture with yogurt and chill before serving. Yield: 3 servings.

♥ FRUIT COTTAGE CHEESE SALAD ♥

1 (3-oz.) pkg. gelatin, any flavor
2 c. cottage cheese
¾ c. vanilla yogurt
¾ c. powdered milk

1 (8-oz.) can pineapple, drained and
crushed
1 (11-oz.) can mandarin oranges
1 (8-oz.) ctn. whipped topping

Pour dry gelatin over cottage cheese. Stir in yogurt, milk, pineapple, oranges and whipped topping. Refrigerate mixture for 2 hours before serving. Yield: 8 servings.

♥ CHAMPAGNE WISHES SALAD ♥

1 (8-oz.) pkg. cream cheese
¾ c. sugar
1 (20-oz.) can pineapple, drained
and crushed

1 (10-oz.) pkg. frozen strawberries,
thawed with liquid
1 (8-oz.) ctn. whipped topping
2 c. mini marshmallows

In a large bowl beat cream cheese and sugar until creamy. Add drained pineapple and undrained strawberries. Fold in whipped topping and marsh-mallows. Put mixture in 9 x 13-inch pan and freeze. Thaw for about 30 minutes before serving. Yield: 12 servings.

♥ AMBROSIA FOR LOVERS ♥

1 (16-oz.) can fruit cocktail, drained
1 (16-oz.) ctn. sour cream
8 oz. mini marshmallows
1 c. coconut flakes

1 (8-oz.) can pineapple, crushed
and drained (opt.)
1 (11-oz.) can mandarin oranges,
drained (opt.)

Prepare this dish at least one day before you plan to serve it. In a large bowl combine fruit cocktail, sour cream and marshmallows. Mix well and sprinkle coconut on top. Top with pineapple and oranges as desired. Yield: 8 servings.

♥ MELON JULEP ♥

2 tsp. orange peel, shredded
2 tsp. lime peel, shredded
½ c. orange juice
½ c. lime juice
2-4 T. sugar

2 T. fresh mint, chopped
8 c. melon balls (watermelon,
cantaloupe, honeydew or favorite)
1 c. lemon-lime carbonated soda,
chilled

Combine peels, juices, sugar and mint in bowl. Pour over melon balls that have been placed in a large bowl. Chill mixture for at least 2 hours. Just before serving pour soda over fruit. Garnish with extra mint sprigs. Yield: 8 (1-cup) servings.

♥ CARAMEL APPLE SWEETHEART SALAD ♥

3 med. apples   **3 chocolate-caramel candy bars**
1 (8-oz.) ctn. whipped topping

Cut unpeeled apples into small pieces. Slice candy bars into thin pieces and mix with apples in a large bowl with the whipped topping. Refrigerate mixture for 4 hours before serving. Yield: 6 servings.

EXTRA FLAVORS, EXTRA FUN

Side Dishes

Handy Household Hints

*A short reference of tried and
true tips for the kitchen*

Competence in the kitchen doesn't always come easy. As a beginning chef, there are probably a lot of things you don't know. Never fear, you can find countless tips and hints in magazines and at your local library. Below is a list of some good ideas to start with.

- Always heat a frying pan before adding butter or oil and sprinkle salt into the pan to prevent spattering.
- Place wax paper underneath ice cube trays to keep them from sticking to the freezer shelf.
- Coffee should be kept in an airtight container in the freezer so the flavor lasts longer.
- Milk won't burn if you sprinkle a teaspoon of sugar into it before boiling.
- Avoid spattering when using an electric mixer by placing the mixing bowl in the sink or punching holes in a paper plate and threading the beaters through the holes.
- A bit of vinegar added to water will keep eggs from cracking as they boil.
- Crystallized honey can be microwaved or set in a pan of hot water for a few seconds to restore freshness.
- To prevent brown sugar from hardening, keep it in the freezer. If it's already too hard, put sliced apples, a couple of marshmallows or a slice of bread in the bag and let it sit for a day or two. If that still doesn't work, grate the sugar on a cheese grater instead of letting it go to waste.
- Ice cream scoops or cookie scoops will help make uniform dollops of batter for muffins and cookies. Baked goods cook more evenly when they're close in size.
- Chicken and other meats are easier to cut when partially frozen.
- After handling fish, wash your hands with lemon juice or vinegar to remove odors. After handling garlic or onions, rub your hands with fresh ginger.
- Soup often tastes better when thickened with instant mashed potatoes instead of flour.
- Never store apples and carrots together because apples emit a gas that gives carrots a bitter taste. However, apples can be stored with potatoes to keep them from sprouting.

Extra Flavors, Extra Fun

♥ BUBBLING OVER BAKED BEANS ♥

1 (32-oz.) can pork and beans
½ med. onion, diced
⅛ c. brown sugar or molasses

2 T. spicy mustard
2 dashes Worcestershire sauce
Crumbled bacon (opt.)

Combine all ingredients on an aluminum roasting pan. Bake at 350° for 40 to 50 minutes. Yield: 10 to 12 servings.

♥ ALMOND GREEN BEANS ♥

4 c. fresh or 2 (10-oz.) pkgs. frozen cut green beans
½ tsp. dill weed
1 tsp. dry mustard

½ lb. pasteurized processed cheese, cubed
½ c. toasted almonds, sliced

In a saucepan cook beans with dill weed until beans are tender; drain. Add mustard and cheese to beans and mix lightly. Place mixture in a 1-quart casserole dish and bake at 350° for 15 minutes. Stir and top with nuts before serving. Yield: 6 to 8 servings.

♥ FAMILY FAVORTE GREEN ♥ BEAN CASSEROLE

1 lb. hamburger
Desired spices
1 (15-oz.) can green beans, drained with some juice reserved

1 (10½-oz.) can tomato soup
Mashed potatoes

In skillet brown hamburger and season with desired spices. Drain grease and mix hamburger with beans and soup. Place contents in casserole dish with mashed potatoes spread on top. Bake at 350° for 20 to 30 minutes or until mixture bubbles and potatoes turn brown. Yield: 6 servings.

♥ SPICY NACHO POTATO TOPPER ♥

1 (10¹/₂-oz.) can Cheddar cheese
  soup, undiluted

¹/₂ c. chunky salsa
4 baked potatoes, hot

In a small sauce pan mix soup and salsa. Cook over low heat, stirring often, until heated through. Split top of baked potatoes. Fluff potatoes and serve with cheese sauce on top. Yield: 4 servings.

♥ BROCCOLI POTATO TOPPER ♥

1 (10¹/₂-oz.) can Cheddar cheese
  soup, undiluted

1 c. broccoli florets, cooked
4 baked potatoes, hot

Stir soup until smooth. Place split potatoes on a microwave safe plate and fluff potatoes with a fork. Top each potato with broccoli florets and spoon soup over top. Microwave topped potatoes on high for 4 minutes or until hot and serve. Yield: 4 servings.

♥ FOILED GRILLED POTATOES ♥

¹/₂ c. mayonnaise
3 cloves garlic, chopped
¹/₂ tsp. paprika
¹/₄ tsp. salt

¹/₄ tsp. pepper
3 potatoes
1 lg. onion

In a large bowl combine mayonnaise, garlic, paprika, salt and pepper. Slice potatoes and onions into ¹/₄-inch thick slices and combine with mayonnaise mixture. Divide mixture evenly among six (12-inch) pieces of tin foil. Seal foil to form a packet and grill for 25 to 30 minutes. Yield: 6 servings.

♥ SKILLET SPUDS ♥

4 slices bacon, cut into ¹/₄ to
  ¹/₂-inch slices
1 onion, diced

3 potatoes, cut into ¹/₄ to ³/₈-inch
  slices
Salt, pepper and oregano to taste

In skillet fry bacon and onion until about half done. Add potatoes and fry mixture until slightly browned. Add enough boiling water to make mixture slightly soupy and add desired spices. Continue cooking for about 10 to 15 minutes before serving. Yield: 4 to 6 servings.

♥ MASHED POTATO CAKES ♥

2 c. mashed potatoes
1 egg, beaten
Flour

Bacon grease
Salad oil

Mix mashed potatoes and egg. Shape mixture into small patties. Flour both sides of patty and fry in 1 part bacon grease and 1 part salad oil in skillet until brown and crisp. Yield: 4 servings.

♥ LOVIN' OVEN FRIES ♥

4 sm. (1 lb.) baking potatoes
1 T. butter, melted
¼ c. Parmesan cheese, grated
½ tsp. garlic salt

½ tsp. paprika
⅛ tsp. onion powder (opt.)
Non-stick cooking spray

Scrub potatoes thoroughly and cut each potato lengthwise into 8 slices. Brush cut surface lightly with melted butter. In a plastic bag combine Parmesan cheese, garlic salt, paprika and onion powder. Add potato slices to bag and shake to coat. Spray an 11 x 7 x 1½-inch baking pan with non-stick cooking spray. Arrange potatoes in baking pan and bake uncovered in a 400° oven for 25 to 30 minutes or until tender. Serve hot. Yield: 3 to 4 servings.

♥ STEAMIN' STUFFED POTATOES ♥

6 baking potatoes
1 (8-oz.) pkg. cream cheese
1 (4-oz.) can deviled ham

1 tsp. onion flakes
3-4 T. mayonnaise
Paprika

Wrap each potato in foil and bake in 400° oven for 1 hour and 15 minutes. In a bowl combine softened cream cheese, ham, onion flakes and mayonnaise and set aside. Unwrap baked potatoes and allow them to cool to touch before cutting in half. Carefully scoop out pulp, leaving shells intact. Combine potato pulp with cream cheese mixture and whip until smooth. Scoop mixture back into shells and sprinkle with paprika. Bake at 350° for 15 to 20 minutes. Yield: 6 servings.

"Cooking is like love. It should be entered into with abandon or not at all."

--Harriet Van Horne

♥ PEAS AND POTATOES ♥

1½ lbs. (about 15) tiny potatoes
Salted water
1-1½ c. fresh peas
3 T. green onion, sliced

4 tsp. butter
4 tsp. flour
1 c. milk

Scrub potatoes and pare off narrow strip of peel around center of each one. Cook potatoes in boiling salted water for 15 to 20 minutes and drain. Meanwhile, cook peas and onions in a small amount of boiling salted water for 8 to 15 minutes and drain. In a saucepan melt butter and stir in flour. Add milk and stir over medium heat until thick. Combine sauce with vegetables and serve. Yield: 4 to 6 servings.

♥ MASHED POTATOES ♥

3 med. (1 lb.) potatoes
2 T. butter

Salt and pepper to taste
Milk

Pare and quarter potatoes. Cook, covered, in a small amount of boiling salted water for 20 to 25 minutes or until tender; drain. Mash with a potato masher or beat with an electric mixer on low speed. Add butter, salt and pepper and gradually beat in enough milk to make light and fluffy. Yield: 4 servings.

♥ PERFECT PAIR PAN GRAVY ♥

Pan drippings from any meat
¼ c. flour

Milk
Salt and pepper to taste

After transferring meat to a serving platter, pour pan drippings and any browned bits into a large measuring cup. Skim drippings and reserve fat. Place ¼ cup of the fat in a medium saucepan and discard the remaining fat. In saucepan stir in flour. Add enough milk to remaining drippings to equal 2 cups. Add liquid to flour mixture all at once. Cook and stir ingredients over medium heat until thick and bubbly. Cook and stir 1 minute more. Salt and pepper to taste. Yield: 4 to 5 servings.

"Be plain in dress, and sober in your diet;
In short, my deary, kiss me and be quiet."
--Lady Mary Wortley Montagu

♥ HOMEMADE HASH BROWNS ♥

1½ lbs. (4 med.) baking potatoes,
  scrubbed and pared
2 T. onion, chopped

¾ tsp. salt
⅛ tsp. pepper
3 T. butter flavor shortening

Shred potatoes into cold water and drain well. Combine with onion, salt and pepper in medium mixing bowl. Melt shortening in large skillet. Spread potatoes evenly in skillet and cook over medium-high heat for 13 to 15 minutes or until golden brown and tender. Turn potatoes with spatula after half the time to keep them from burning. Yield: 4 to 6 servings.

♥ PEAS IN A POD & CARROTS ♥

¾ c. water
2 c. baby carrots
1 (8-oz.) pkg. fresh pea pods,
  washed and cleaned

3 T. butter
½ tsp. cornstarch
2 tsp. honey

In a 2-quart saucepan bring water to a full boil. Add carrots. Cover and cook 10 to 12 minutes over medium heat until carrots are crisp-tender. Add pea pods. Continue cooking 1 to 2 minutes until pea pods are crisp-tender. Drain and set aside. In the same pan melt butter and stir in cornstarch. Add carrots, pea pods and honey. Cook 2 to 3 minutes over medium heat, stirring occasionally, until heated through. Yield: 4 to 6 servings.

♥ SIDE BY SIDE SAVORY PEAS ♥

1 onion
3 T. butter
1 T. flour
1 (15-oz.) can peas, with ½ c. liquid
  reserved

1 T. parsley, chopped
Dash thyme
1 bay leaf

Slice onion and separate into rings. Cook in boiling water until tender; drain. Brown onions in butter. Add flour and blend. Add peas, pea liquid, parsley, thyme and bay leaf. Heat to serving temperature. Remove bay leaf and serve. Yield: 4 servings.

♥ LOVE YA BABY CARROTS ♥

1 (16-oz.) pkg. baby carrots, pared
2 tsp. butter
2 tsp. brown sugar

2-3 T. pineapple juice
½ T. ground ginger
Chopped parsley

Cook carrots in small amount of boiling water for 5 minutes or until carrots are crisp-tender; drain. Melt butter in a small saucepan. Add brown sugar, pineapple juice and ginger. Pour liquid over carrots. Garnish with parsley and serve. Yield: 4 to 6 servings.

♥ GLAZED CARROTS ♥

1 lb. carrots, pared and sliced
1 T. liquid margarine
1 T. Dijon mustard
2 T. honey

1 tsp. lemon zest
¼ tsp. white pepper
¼ tsp. ginger

Steam carrots until tender-crisp. In a small pan combine remaining ingredients over low heat, stirring until just combined. Pour sauce over carrots and toss gently to coat before serving. Yield: 4 to 6 servings.

♥ FRIED ONION RINGS ♥

¾ c. all-purpose flour
⅔ c. milk
1 egg
1 T. oil
¼ tsp. salt

Shortening or oil for deep-fat
  frying
4 med. mild yellow or white onions,
  sliced ¼ inch thick

In a bowl combine flour, milk, egg, oil and salt. Beat until just smooth. In a large skillet heat 1 inch of shortening or oil to 375°. Separate onions into rings. Using a fork, dip onion rings into batter and drain off excess. Fry onion rings, a few at a time, in a single layer in hot oil 2 to 3 minutes or until golden brown, stirring occasionally to separate rings. Remove from oil and drain on paper towels. Keep fried rings warm in a 300° oven while frying remaining rings. Yield: 4 to 6 servings.

"Happiness is good health and a bad memory."
--Ingride Bergman

♥ EGGPLANT PARMIGIANA ♥

1 (³/₄-lb.) eggplant
1 egg, beaten
¹/₄ c. all-purpose flour
2 T. cooking oil

¹/₃ c. Parmesan cheese, grated
1 c. spaghetti sauce
1 c. mozzarella cheese, shredded

Peel eggplant and cut crosswise into ¹/₂-inch-thick slices. Dip eggplant into egg, then into flour, turning to coat both sides. In a large skillet cook eggplant, half at a time, in hot oil for 4 to 6 minutes or until golden, turning once. Drain on paper towels. Place eggplant slices in a single layer in a 12 x 7¹/₂ x 2-inch baking dish, cutting slices to fit. Sprinkle with Parmesan. Top with spaghetti sauce and mozzarella. Bake in a 400° oven 10 to 12 minutes or until hot. Yield: 4 servings.

♥ STIR FRY VEGGIES ♥

¹/₂ lb. broccoli
¹/₂ lb. zucchini
¹/₂ lb. carrots
3 oz. onions
3 oz. mushrooms
1¹/₂ T. olive oil

1 sm. clove garlic, crushed
¹/₂ tsp. salt
¹/₂ tsp. pepper
¹/₂ T. Italian seasoning
¹/₂ T. soy sauce

Cut broccoli into 1-inch pieces. Cut zucchini and carrots into ¹/₂-inch slices and onion and mushrooms into ¹/₄-inch slices. In a wok or large frying pan heat oil with garlic, salt, pepper and Italian seasonings. Add vegetables and cook, stirring constantly, until vegetables are crisp-tender. Stir in soy sauce and serve. Yield: 8 servings.

♥ ACORN SQUASH ♥

1 lg. acorn squash
2 tsp. brown sugar

1 tsp. butter

Microwave whole squash 3 minutes. Remove from microwave and cut in half lengthwise. Scoop out seeds. In each half of squash place 1 teaspoon brown sugar and ¹/₂ teaspoon butter. Cover each squash with small paper plate and set in microwave safe bowl. Microwave each half 10 minutes or until tender. Yield: 2 servings.

♥ CANDIED YAMS ♥

3-4 lg. sweet potatoes
2 c. sugar
½ c. milk
½ c. margarine

Cut potatoes in long French fry shape strips. Put potatoes in a 9 x 13-inch baking dish. Pour sugar and milk over potatoes. Cut butter in slices, placing over potatoes. Bake in 450° oven for about 1 hour. Yield: 4 to 6 servings.

♥ TOMATO-ZUCCHINI PIE ♥

2 c. zucchini, chopped
1 c. tomato, chopped
½ c. onion, chopped
⅓ c. Parmesan cheese, grated
1½ c. milk
¾ c. baking mix
3 eggs
½ tsp. salt
¼ tsp. pepper
Tomato slices

In a greased 10-inch pie plate sprinkle zucchini, tomato, onion and Parmesan. In a separate bowl beat together milk, baking mix, eggs, salt and pepper until smooth. Pour into pie plate. Bake in preheated 400° oven for 30 minutes or until knife comes out clean. Cool 5 minutes. Garnish with fresh tomato slices and serve. Yield: 6 servings.

♥ STUFFED ZUCCHINI FOR TWO ♥

2 (6-inch) zucchinis
¼ c. carrots, diced
¼ c. peas, frozen or fresh
Pinch garlic powder
½ dry bread crumbs
¼ c. tomatoes, peeled and diced
⅛ tsp. poultry seasoning
¼ tsp. parsley flakes
⅛ tsp. salt
Pinch pepper
1 T. water
2 T. Parmesan cheese, grated

Cut unpeeled zucchini in half lengthwise. Boil in salted water for 5 minutes; drain. Scoop out seeds and discard. Cook carrots, peas and garlic powder in a small amount of water until tender; drain. Mix crumbs, tomatoes, poultry seasoning, parsley flakes, salt and pepper together. Stir in water. Add to carrots and peas; stir. Stuff zucchini shells with carrot and pea mixture. Sprinkle with grated Parmesan. Bake in 350° oven for 20 minutes or until heated through. Yield: 2 servings.

♥ HOT STUFF JALAPEÑO ♥
CORN CASSEROLE

1 T. olive oil
2-3 jalapeño chilies, seeded and
  chopped
1 onion, chopped
1 red bell pepper, seeded and
  chopped
4 c. fresh or frozen corn

1 c. cottage cheese
1 egg
2 egg whites
1 T. cornstarch
½ tsp. celery seed
½ c. Cheddar cheese, grated

Heat olive oil in a medium skillet. Sauté chilies, onion and bell pepper until tender. Mix in 2 cups corn. In blender combine remaining corn, cottage cheese, egg, egg whites, cornstarch and celery seed. Process 1 to 2 minutes or until smooth. Combine corn mixture with sautéed vegetables. Pour into a 9 x 13-inch baking dish that has been coated with cooking spray. Sprinkle with cheese. Bake at 375° for about 30 minutes or until mixture puffs in center. Yield: 10 to 12 servings.

♥ CUDDLY CORN CASSEROLE ♥

1 (15-oz.) can cream corn
1 (15-oz.) can kernel corn, drained
1½ c. sour cream
½ c. butter
3 eggs, beaten

1 (8½-oz.) box cornbread mix
¾ c. onion, chopped
¾ c. green pepper, chopped
2 c. Cheddar cheese, shredded

In a large bowl mix all ingredients together. Pour into a greased 9 x 13-inch pan and bake at 350° for 45 minutes. Mixture is done when toothpick inserted in center comes out clean. Yield: 10 to 12 servings.

♥ MELT YOUR HEART MACARONI ♥

1 c. elbow macaroni, uncooked
1 (15-oz.) can cream corn
1 (15-oz.) can whole kernel corn,
  undrained

1 c. pasteurized processed cheese,
  cubed

Put uncooked macaroni in casserole dish. Pour both cans of corn over the top. Add processed cheese. Cover dish with aluminum foil. Cook in oven for 1 hour at 350°. Yield: 6 servings.

♥ SWEET STUFF RED CABBAGE ♥

2 T. olive oil
1 head red cabbage, cored and
　shredded
1 onion, chopped
2 apples, cored and diced but
　unpeeled

½ c. dry red wine or red wine
　vinegar
2 bay leaves
⅓ c. red currant jelly
Water

Heat olive oil in a large skillet. Add and sauté cabbage, onion and apples,
stirring often, for about 5 to 10 minutes or until mixture is wilted. Add
remaining ingredients. Cover pan and simmer for 15 to 20 minutes. Add water
as needed to prevent cabbage from sticking. Remove bay leaves and serve.
Yield: 6 to 8 servings.

♥ BRUSSELS SPROUTS ♥

2 c. fresh chestnuts
Water
2 c. Brussels sprouts
1 c. chicken broth, defatted

1 T. caraway seeds
1 T. kümmel, caraway flavored
　liqueur (opt.)
¼ tsp. white pepper

Cut an "X" in the bottom of each chestnut. Place in saucepan. Cover with
water and simmer for 5 minutes. Remove from water and peel shell and skin
from each chestnut; set aside. Steam Brussels sprouts until tender-crisp and
set aside. Combine chestnuts and broth in a skillet. Simmer for about 10
minutes or until chestnuts are tender. Add caraway seeds and simmer for
about 5 minutes or until broth is reduced by half. Add Brussels sprouts,
kümmel and pepper. Stir until heated through and serve. Yield: 6 servings.

♥ BROCCOLI CASSEROLE ♥

1 (16-oz.) pkg. frozen broccoli,
　chopped
1 (15-oz.) can cream corn

2 eggs, beaten
2 T. butter

In saucepan boil broccoli until tender and drain. Add cream corn, eggs and
butter. Mix well and place ingredients in a casserole dish. Bake mixture at
350° for 20 to 25 minutes. Yield: 6 servings.

♥ SPICY ORANGE BROCCOLI ♥

1 lb. broccoli, trimmed
1 c. fresh orange juice
1 T. cornstarch
1 tsp. orange zest
$^1/_2$ tsp. dried tarragon or $^1/_8$ tsp.
  red pepper flakes

$^1/_2$ tsp. dry mustard
2-3 drops hot pepper sauce
Fresh parsley or chives, chopped

Cut broccoli into spears and steam until tender-crisp. Keep warm while preparing sauce. In a small saucepan blend orange juice gradually into cornstarch. Add zest, tarragon, mustard and hot pepper sauce. Cook over low heat, stirring constantly, until thickened. Serve sauce over broccoli and garnish with parsley or chives and additional orange zest. Yield: 6 servings.

♥ STIR-FRIED BROCCOLI ♥

2 tsp. oriental sesame oil
1 clove garlic, minced
1 T. fresh ginger, minced
4 green onions, thinly sliced
$^1/_2$ lb. mushrooms, sliced
1 lb. broccoli, cut into florets
$^1/_3$ c. peanuts, almonds or cashews
  (opt.)

1 (8-oz.) can water chestnuts, sliced
1 T. cornstarch
1 tsp. brown sugar
$^3/_4$ c. chicken broth, defatted
2 tsp. soy sauce

Heat wok and add oil. Swirl to coat entire surface with oil. Add garlic, ginger, green onions and mushrooms. Stir-fry for 2 to 3 minutes. Do not let garlic burn. Add broccoli, nuts and water chestnuts and stir-fry for 3 to 4 minutes. In a separate bowl combine cornstarch and brown sugar. Gradually add chicken broth and then stir in soy sauce. Pour broth mixture into broccoli mixture in wok. Cook and stir until thickened. Reduce heat and simmer, covered, until broccoli is tender-crisp, or for about 5 minutes. Serve immediately. Yield: 6 to 8 servings.

♥ STEAMED OVEN RICE PILAF ♥

1 c. whole-grain wild rice
2 T. butter
$1^1/_2$ T. minced onions
1 (4-oz.) can mushroom stems and
  pieces

$^1/_4$ c. sliced almonds
1 ($10^1/_2$-oz.) can condensed beef
  broth
$^2/_3$ c. water

Preheat oven to 350°. Combine rice, butter, minced onions, mushrooms and almonds in a greased $1^1/_2$-quart casserole dish. Heat broth and water to boiling. Pour into casserole dish, stir, cover and bake for 30 minutes or until rice is tender and all liquid is absorbed. Yield: 4 servings.

♥ SPANISH RICE ♥

³⁄₄ lb. ground chuck	1 c. long-grain wild rice, uncooked
¹⁄₂ c. onion, chopped	¹⁄₂ tsp. salt
¹⁄₂ c. green pepper, chopped	¹⁄₄ tsp. pepper
1 (16-oz.) can whole tomatoes	¹⁄₂ tsp. Worcestershire sauce
1 (12-oz.) can vegetable juice	

Combine ground chuck, onion and green pepper in pan. Cook over low heat, stirring occasionally until meat is brown and vegetables soft; drain fat. Add tomatoes, vegetable juice, rice, salt, pepper and Worcestershire sauce and bring to a boil. Cook 25 minutes, stirring occasionally until liquid is mostly absorbed. Yield: 4 to 6 servings.

♥ FETTUCCINE FOR A COUPLE ♥

1 pkg. instant chicken broth mix	1 red or green pepper, cut in strips
¹⁄₄ c. water	1 zucchini, cut in strips
2 carrots, chopped	4¹⁄₂ oz. fettuccine, cooked
	2 T. margarine

Dissolve broth mix in water. Add carrots and microwave on high 3 to 4 minutes. Add pepper and zucchini. Microwave another 3 to 4 minutes, stirring halfway. Mix with fettuccine and margarine, tossing gently. Yield: 2 servings.

♥ VEGGIE RAGOUT ♥

1 T. olive or vegetable oil	¹⁄₄ tsp. pepper
1 tsp. fresh garlic, finely chopped	2 T. fresh basil leaves, chopped
4 med. ripe Roma tomatoes, cut into wedges	2 T. fresh parsley, chopped
3 c. eggplant, peeled and cubed	1 (15¹⁄₂-oz.) can butter beans, rinsed and drained
1 c. zucchini, sliced	1 (15¹⁄₂-oz.) can dark red kidney beans, rinsed and drained
1 c. summer squash, sliced	¹⁄₄ c. Romano or Parmesan cheese, freshly grated
1 sm. onion, sliced	
¹⁄₂ red pepper, cut into strips	
¹⁄₄ tsp. salt	

Heat oil in a 10-inch skillet and add garlic. Cook 2 to 3 minutes over medium-high heat, stirring constantly, until garlic is browned. Add tomatoes, eggplant, zucchini, squash, onion, red pepper, salt, pepper, basil and parsley. Cover and continue cooking for 20 to 25 minutes, stirring occasionally, until vegetables are tender. Uncover and continue cooking 5 to 7 minutes to reduce liquid. Gently stir in beans. Continue cooking 2 to 3 minutes until beans are heated through. Serve with Romano or Parmesan cheese. Yield: 6 servings.

♥ VALENTINE RED BEANS AND RICE ♥

½ lb. bacon
2 (15-oz.) cans red beans
2 c. onion, chopped
1 c. green onion, chopped
Parsley
½ T. garlic salt
1 T. Worcestershire sauce
½ T. hot pepper sauce
½ tsp. red pepper, crushed
½ tsp. black pepper
¼ tsp. oregano
1 lb. sausage, cut up
1 (8-oz.) can tomato sauce
Yellow rice, cooked

Cook bacon; drain. In a large skillet or pan combine all other ingredients and simmer 1 hour. Serve over yellow rice. Yield: 8 servings.

♥ HOT & SPICY CHILI-CHEESE RICE ♥

1 (6-oz.) can whole green chilies
¾ c. rice, uncooked
1 c. sour cream
Salt and pepper to taste
1 (8-oz.) pkg. Monterey Jack cheese, shredded
Butter

Split open chilies and remove seeds. Cook rice. Mix with sour cream; salt and pepper to taste. In a casserole dish layer rice, cheese, chilies, rice and cheese. Dot with butter. Bake at 350° for 30 minutes. Yield: 4 to 6 servings.

♥ RIGATONI FOR TWO ♥

2 oz. chicken breast
Flour
2 T. olive oil
1 c. broccoli florets
¼ tsp. garlic, chopped
1 slice lemon
¼ c. chicken broth
¾ c. heavy cream or white wine
2 c. rigatoni, cooked

Cut chicken into 6 strips and dust in flour. In a skillet brown floured chicken strips in oil. Add broccoli, garlic and lemon. Cook and stir 1 minute. Add chicken broth and cream. Cook until boiling, reduce heat by half and simmer a few minutes until thickened. Add rigatoni and cook about 2 minutes or until heated. Yield: 2 servings.

"There is only one happiness in life, to love and be loved."
--George Sand

♥ IN PERFECT HARMONY QUICHE ♥

1 (9-in.) pre-made pie crust
1 (4-oz.) can mushrooms, drained
½ c. ham, diced
4 oz. Swiss cheese, shredded
1 T. flour

¼ tsp. salt
⅛ tsp. nutmeg
3 eggs, beaten
1 c. milk

Thaw crust at room temperature, about 20 minutes if frozen. Place thawed crust in a pie plate and spread mushrooms and ham over bottom. Sprinkle cheese on top. Stir together flour, salt, nutmeg, eggs and milk. Pour over cheese. Bake per crust instructions. Let stand 10 minutes before serving. Yield: 6 servings.

♥ LOVEABLE LINGUINI ♥

16 oz. linguini
6 oz. butter

4 oz. lemon juice, freshly squeezed
¾ c. fresh parsley

Boil linguini in salted water, as package directs. Melt butter and mix with lemon juice. Pour over cooked linguini. Garnish with fresh parsley and serve. Yield: 4 servings.

♥ TEMPTING FETTUCCINE ALFREDO ♥

3 T. light or whipping cream
1 (4-oz.) pkg. fettuccine
⅓ c. Parmesan cheese, grated

1 T. margarine
Black pepper, coarsely cracked
Nutmeg, ground

Let cream come to room temperature. Cook fettuccini according to package directions; drain well. Return fettuccine to the hot saucepan. Add cream, Parmesan and margarine. Toss gently until fettuccine is well coated. Transfer to a warm serving dish. Sprinkle with pepper and nutmeg. Serve immediately. Yield: 4 servings.

"There is no more lovely, friendly and charming relation-ship, communion or company than a good marriage.
--Martin Luther

♥ SO SAUCY SPAGHETTI SAUCE ♥

1 lb. ground beef or pork
1 1/2 c. fresh mushrooms, sliced
1/2 c. onion, chopped
1/2 c. green pepper, chopped
2 cloves garlic, minced
2 (16-oz.) cans tomatoes, cut up and
  undrained
1 (6-oz.) can tomato paste

1 tsp. sugar
1 tsp. dried oregano, crushed
1 tsp. dried basil, crushed
1 tsp. dried thyme, crushed
1 bay leaf
1/2 tsp. salt
1/4 tsp. pepper
6 c. spaghetti, cooked and hot

In a large skillet cook meat, mushrooms, onion, green pepper and garlic until meat is brown; drain. Stir in undrained tomatoes, tomato paste, sugar, oregano, basil, thyme, bay leaf, salt and pepper. Bring to boil and reduce heat. Cover and simmer 30 minutes. Uncover and simmer 10 to 15 minutes more or to desired consistency, stirring occasionally. Discard bay leaf and serve over spaghetti. Yield: 6 servings.

♥ PASTA BELLA STIR-FRY ♥

2 c. broccoli florets
1 c. carrots, sliced
1/4 c. margarine
2 c. summer squash, sliced
1/2 lb. fresh asparagus spears, cut
  into 1/2-inch pieces
3/4 lb. pasteurized processed cheese,
  cubed

3/4 c. half-and-half
1/2 tsp. dried oregano, crushed
2 c. (4-oz.) bow tie noodles, cooked
  and drained
1/3 c. Parmesan cheese, grated
1/4 lb. pepperoni, chicken or ham,
  cubed (opt.)

In large skillet or wok stir-fry broccoli and carrots in margarine for 3 minutes. Add squash and asparagus and stir-fry until crisp-tender. Reduce to medium heat and add processed cheese, half-and-half and oregano. Stir until melted. Add remaining ingredients and mix lightly. If desired you may add pepperoni, chicken or ham cubes. Yield: 6 servings.

♥ YOU'RE THE BEST PRIMA PASTA ♥

1 head cauliflower
1 bunch broccoli
3 zucchini squash
Handful snow peas (opt.)
3 tomatoes

1 (16-oz.) pkg. large shell macaroni
1/2 c. butter
2-3 whole garlic cloves, mashed
1 c. half-and-half (opt.)
1 c. Romano cheese, grated (opt.)

Slice or floret vegetables and set aside. Cook macaroni and drain. In a large skillet melt butter. Add garlic and vegetables and sauté. Cover and cook 2 to 3 minutes. Mix pasta and vegetables together. If desired, add half-and-half and then grated Romano. Serve warm or cold. Yield: 8 servings.

♥ CUDDLE UP CLAM LINGUINI ♥

1 (16-oz.) pkg. angel hair pasta
2 T. butter
2 cloves garlic, minced
1 bunch green onions, sliced
1 (4-oz.) can sliced mushrooms,
  drained

1 (10-oz.) can minced clams,
  drained
1 T. flour
$\frac{1}{2}$ c. sour cream
Salt and pepper to taste
Parmesan cheese to taste

Cook pasta according to package directions. In small skillet melt butter and sauté garlic and green onion. Add mushrooms and clams. Stir quickly and sprinkle with flour. Stir until flour is golden and all butter is absorbed. Add sour cream and continue stirring. Reduce heat to warm mixture through. Do not boil the sour cream. Add salt and pepper to taste. Drain pasta and place it in a large bowl. Pour creamed clam sauce over top and sprinkle with Parmesan cheese before serving. Yield: 2 generous or 4 small servings.

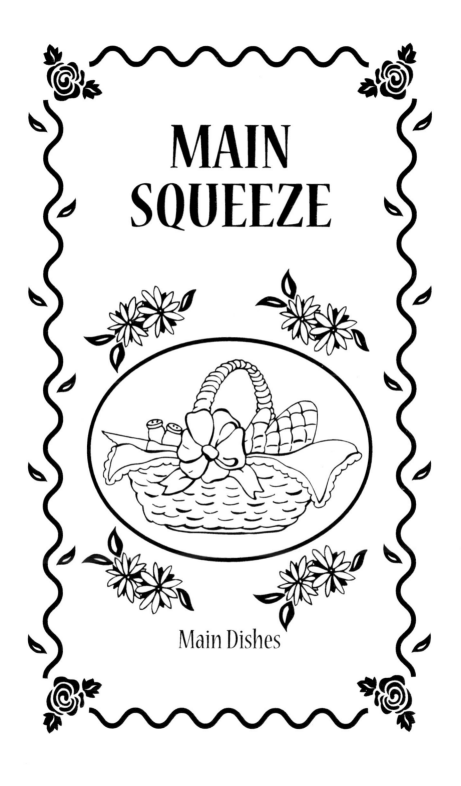

MAIN SQUEEZE

Main Dishes

Homemade Cleaners
A do-it-yourself guide to making everyday cleansers at a fraction of store-bought prices

If you're just starting out, you may think you need to rush out and plunk down tons of money for industrial strength cleansers every time you see a little spill or spot. Just look around your house to find many natural cleansers minus the fancy bottle and big price. For example, a solution of equal parts powdered chalk and baking soda, mixed with water into a paste makes a wonderful metal polisher. Below are a few other hints for whipping up homemade helpers.

- For carpet spills, pour plain club soda on the spot and let it soak for a few seconds before drying it off. For an older stain, combine 2 tablespoons detergent, 3 tablespoons vinegar and 1 quart water. Work it into the stain and blot dry. If that doesn't work, mix bleach free powdered laundry detergent and warm water and brush it into the stain before drying it off.
- To remove water spots from glasses, add 1/2 cup bleach to the dishwashing cycle and 1/2 cup vinegar to the rinse.
- To remove toilet rings, rub them gently with a wet pumice stone.
- For a window cleaning solution, mix 1/3 to 1/2 cup ammonia, 1 cup white vinegar and 2 tablespoons cornstarch into a bucket of warm water.
- To clean dirty brass objects, boil them for several hours in a pan of water mixed with 1 tablespoon salt and 1 cup white vinegar. For lacquered or varnished brass, apply a paste of lemon juice and cream of tartar. Leave for 5 minutes and wash in warm water.
- Artificial flowers can be cleaned by shaking them in a paper bag with a little salt.
- White clothes that have yellowed can be helped by a solution of 2 gallons hot water, 1/2 cup automatic dishwasher detergent and 1/4 cup liquid bleach. Soak the clothing for half an hour, wash and rinse in water mixed with 1/2 cup white vinegar.
- For an all-purpose cleanser mix 1/2 teaspoon liquid soap with 2 tablespoons lemon juice, 1/2 teaspoon washing soda, 1 teaspoon borax and 2 cups hot water. For tough stains, mix 1/2 cup ammonia, 1/2 cup washing soda and 1/2 gallon warm water.
- Unclog drains by pouring in 1/2 cup baking soda followed by 1/2 cup vinegar. Plug drain and allow ingredients to set for about 15 minutes before flushing with cold water. Repeat steps, this time using 1/2 cup salt and 1/2 cup boiling water. Let set 15 minutes before flushing with cold water.

Main Squeeze

Beloved Beef

♥ MOIST BEEF ROAST ♥

1 (10½-oz.) can French onion soup
  or 1 pkg. dry onion soup mix and
  1 c. water

1 (10½-oz.) can cream of
  mushroom soup
2-3 lbs. beef roast

Pour soups or soup mix and water over the roast, cover and bake at 350° for 2½ to 3 hours. You may use an oven roasting bag if desired. Yield: 6 to 8 servings with leftovers.

♥ PERFECT POT ROAST ♥

Salt and pepper to taste
2¼ lbs. boneless chuck roast
4 potatoes, pared and halved
4 onions, peeled

3 carrots, sliced
1 pkg. sloppy joe mix
1 (6-oz.) can tomato juice

Place foil in a shallow roasting pan. Salt and pepper beef and place on foil. Surround with vegetables. Combine sloppy joe mixture with tomato juice and pour liquid over roast. Wrap and seal roast in foil and cook in preheated 400° oven for 1 hour and 10 minutes. Remove from oven and allow to stand in wrap for 30 minutes before serving. Yield: 4 to 6 servings.

♥ MEAT LOAF DIVINE ♥

2 lbs. ground chuck
1 pkg. dry onion soup mix
1½ c. soft bread crumbs

2 eggs
⅓ c. ketchup
¾ c. water

Preheat oven to 375°. In a large bowl combine all ingredients and mix well. Form into a loaf and place in loaf pan. Bake for 45 to 50 minutes. Yield: 6 to 8 servings.

♥ BEEF STROGANOFF ♥

1-1½ lbs. beef, cubed
Flour
2 T. fat
1 med. onion, chopped
2 (6-oz.) cans mushrooms, sliced,
  with juice

1 (10½-oz.) can tomato soup
1 c. sour cream
1 clove garlic or 1 tsp. garlic salt
Rice, cooked

Dredge beef in flour and brown in fat in a skillet. Mix together beef, onion, mushrooms, soup, sour cream and garlic. Bake mixture in a greased casserole dish at 325° to 350° for 2 hours. Serve over rice. Yield: 4 to 6 servings.

♥ EXTRAVAGANT BEEF BRISKET ♥

1 pkg. dry onion soup mix
¾ c. water
½ c. ketchup

1 tsp. garlic powder
½ tsp. black pepper
3 lbs. beef brisket

Preheat oven to 325°. In a 13 x 9-inch baking or roasting pan, mix onion soup mix with water, ketchup, garlic powder and pepper. Add brisket, turning to coat with soup mixture. Loosely cover with foil and roast for 3 hours or until brisket is tender. Thicken sauce into gravy if desired. Yield: 6 to 8 servings.

♥ MARINATED STEAKS, MY DARLING ♥

2 steaks (any kind)
Liquid smoke

Garlic salt to taste
12 T. butter, 6 per steak

Tenderize each steak and rub with liquid smoke. Sprinkle a small amount garlic salt directly onto each steak and work it evenly over the surface. Repeat for other side of steak. Put steaks and liquid in a covered container and shake vigorously for at least 1 minute. Marinate in refrigerator for no less than 5 minutes up to overnight for a richer flavor. When ready to serve, grill steaks and rub butter on each side after turning them over on grill. Yield: 2 servings.

"And love can come to everyone,
The best things in life are free."
--Lew Brown and Buddy De Silva

♥ FLAVORFUL FAJITAS ♥

1 lb. beef round steak, cut into thin
  strips
2 T. oil
1 med. green pepper, cut into strips
1 med. onion, sliced

¹/₄ lb. pasteurized processed
  Mexican cheese, cubed
4 (8-inch) flour tortillas
1 c. tomato, chopped

In large skillet sauté steak in oil for 4 minutes. Add green pepper and onions and mix lightly. Reduce heat to medium. Cook for 5 minutes or until steak is tender; drain. Add processed cheese and stir until melted. Fill tortillas with steak mixture and tomatoes and roll before serving. Yield: 4 servings.

♥ BEEF KABOBS ♥

1 lb. boneless sirloin steak
1 (8-oz.) bottle Russian salad
  dressing
2 T. lemon juice
1 T. Worcestershire sauce
¹/₈ tsp. pepper
¹/₈ tsp. garlic powder

10 slices bacon, halved
2 med. green peppers, cut into
  1¹/₂-inch pieces
1 lg. onion, cut into 1¹/₂-inch pieces
¹/₂ lb. fresh mushrooms
1 pt. cherry tomatoes

Trim fat from meat and cut into 1¹/₂-inch cubes. Place meat in a shallow container. In a bowl combine salad dressing, lemon juice, Worcestershire sauce, pepper and garlic powder. Pour liquid over meat. Cover and marinate in refrigerator for at least 8 hours. Drain and reserve marinade. Wrap bacon around meat and secure with wooden toothpick. Alternate meat and vegetables on 4 skewers. Grill kabob skewers over medium to hot coals, turning and basting frequently with marinade reserve, for 15 minutes or until meat is tender. Yield: 4 servings.

♥ SWISS STEAK ♥

2 lbs. inexpensive steak
1 pkg. dry onion soup mix
1 green pepper
1 (16-oz.) can tomatoes, drained
  with 1 c. juice reserved

1 (8-oz.) can mushrooms
1 T. steak sauce
1 T. cornstarch

Cut steak into serving-sized pieces and put in baking dish or pan. Sprinkle onion soup mix over meat. Cut green peppers into strips and put on top of meat. Drain tomatoes, reserving juice, and put on top of mixture. Drain mushrooms and layer on top. In a bowl mix tomato juice, steak sauce and cornstarch and pour liquid over steak. Cover contents with foil and bake at 375° for 2 hours. Yield: 6 servings.

♥ COMPANY'S COMING PRIME RIB ♥

1 T. dry mustard
1½ tsp. salt
½ tsp. paprika
¼ tsp. allspice
½ tsp. pepper

1 (4 to 5-lb.) prime rib roast, rolled
  and tied
1 sm. onion, slivered
2 cloves garlic, slivered
Fresh parsley

Combine mustard, salt, paprika, allspice and pepper and set aside. Cut long, deep slits about 1 inch apart in top of roast. Stuff each slit with onion, garlic, parsley and a small amount of spice mixture. Rub remaining spice mixture onto roast. Place on a roasting rack and bake for 2 to 2½ hours in a 325° oven. Yield: 8 to 10 servings.

♥ CASSEROLE SURPRISE ♥

1 lb. ground beef
2 c. macaroni
1 (10½-oz.) can tomato soup

1 (10½-oz.) can condensed chili
  beef soup
5 slices American cheese

Brown meat in skillet. Boil macaroni and drain. Add macaroni and soups to meat. Heat together. Put cheese slices on top of mixture. Cover and let cheese melt slightly. Yield: 4 servings.

♥ HAMBURGER CASSEROLE ♥

½ lb. hamburger
2 sm. carrots, sliced
2 med. potatoes, sliced
½ c. onions, diced

1 (10½-oz.) can cream of
  mushroom soup
3 slices American cheese

Press ¾ of the hamburger into the bottom of a greased casserole dish. Layer carrots, potatoes and onions on top. Crumble remaining hamburger over vegetables. Spread soup over all and top with cheese slices. Cover dish with aluminum foil and bake in a preheated 350° oven for at least 1 hour and 15 minutes. Yield: 2 to 4 servings.

"Union gives strength."

--Aesop

♥ EASY & ENDEARING CASSEROLE ♥

1½-2 lbs. stew beef, trimmed
1 (10½-oz.) can golden mushroom
  soup

1 (10½-oz.) can onion soup

Place uncooked beef and soups in casserole dish. Cover and cook in 325° oven for 3 hours or crockpot on low for 8 to 10 hours. Serve over rice or noodles. Yield: 4 to 6 servings.

♥ CROCKPOT CUBED STEAK ♥

1½ lbs. cube steak, cut in pieces
1 pkg. dry onion soup mix

2 (10½-oz.) cans cream of
  mushroom or celery soup
1 soup can water

Put all ingredients in crock pot. Cook on low all day, or about 8 hours. Serve with noodles, rice or mashed potatoes. Yield: 4 servings.

♥ PEPPER STEAK FOR A NIGHT ALONE ♥

1½ lbs. round steak
1 clove garlic, minced
1 c. onion, chopped
½ tsp. salt
¼ tsp. pepper
¼ tsp. ground ginger

1 tsp. sugar
¼ c. soy sauce
1 lg. bell pepper
1 (14½-oz.) can stewed tomatoes
1 T. cornstarch (opt.)
½ c. cold water (opt.)

Brown steak. Put steak and remaining ingredients into a crockpot. Mix and cook on high for 3 to 5 hours. To thicken sauce, mix cornstarch and water and add to other ingredients. Yield: 4 servings.

♥ LOVE ON THE ROLL ♥

1 lb. ground beef
1 sm. onion, chopped
1 c. quick-cooking rice
Water

Cabbage, chopped with 8 outer
  leaves reserved
1 (10½-oz.) can tomato soup

Brown meat and onion in skillet. Drain fat and add rice and water. Cook mixture until rice is done. Add chopped cabbage and cook until slightly tender. Roll mixture in cabbage leaves. Cover with tomato soup and a can of water. Simmer for 30 minutes before serving. Yield: 4 servings.

♥ CRISP HASH FOR MY HONEY ♥

2 T. butter
1 c. beef chuck, cooked and diced
1 c. potato, cooked and diced
1 med. onion, diced

1 T. parsley, minced
$^{1}/_{2}$ c. milk
Salt and pepper to taste

In a heavy skillet melt butter over medium-high heat. Add all remaining ingredients and mix well. Cover and cook until crisp on bottom. Turn and brown other side. Serve immediately. Yield: 2 servings.

♥ SWEETHEART SLOPPY JOES ♥

1$^{1}/_{2}$ lbs. ground beef
1 (10$^{1}/_{2}$-oz.) can cream of chicken
  soup
$^{1}/_{4}$ c. ketchup

Squirt of mustard
$^{1}/_{4}$ c. brown sugar
Hamburger buns

Brown ground beef in a skillet and drain. Add soup, ketchup, mustard and brown sugar and heat, stirring occasionally. Serve on buns. Yield: 4 servings.

♥ STUFFED PEPPERS FOR TWO ♥

2 med. green peppers
Salted water
$^{1}/_{2}$ lb. lean ground beef
$^{1}/_{4}$ c. instant rice, uncooked
1 (8-oz.) can tomato sauce, divided

1 T. onion, chopped
$^{1}/_{2}$ tsp. salt
Dash pepper
$^{1}/_{2}$ tsp. Worcestershire sauce
1 egg, beaten

Cut off top of each pepper and remove seeds. Cook pepper for 5 minutes in enough boiling salted water to cover the top. Drain and set aside. In a bowl combine ground beef, rice, $^{1}/_{4}$ c. tomato sauce, onion, salt, pepper, Worcestershire sauce and egg. Stuff peppers with mixture and place in a small baking pan. Pour remaining tomato sauce over peppers. Cover contents and bake at 350° for 50 to 60 minutes or until meat is done, basting peppers twice with drippings. Yield: 2 servings.

♥ SIMPLE GOULASH ♥

1 pkg. macaroni and cheese
1 lb. ground beef
$^{1}/_{2}$ c. onion, chopped

1 T. chili powder
1 (16-oz.) can tomatoes in juice,
  chopped

Prepare macaroni and cheese according to package directions and set aside. Brown ground beef and onion in skillet. Drain off fat. Stir in chili powder. Add tomatoes and juice and simmer meat mixture for 5 minutes. Pour meat mixture into macaroni and mix well before serving. Yield: 4 servings.

♥ LOVIN' YOU LASAGNE ♥

1 lb. ground beef
1 (32-oz.) jar spaghetti sauce
½ c. water
1 tsp. salt
1 (8-oz.) pkg. lasagne noodles

1 (16-oz.) ctn. sm. curd cottage
  cheese
3 c. mozzarella cheese
½ c. Parmesan Cheese, grated

Cook ground beef and drain well. Add spaghetti sauce, water and salt. Cook several minutes. In microwavable 9 x 13-inch dish layer ½ spaghetti sauce, ½ uncooked noodles, 1 cup cottage cheese and ⅓ mozzarella; repeat layers. End with sauce and cheese. Microwave, covered, for 20 minutes, turning dish several times. Let dish stand 10 minutes before serving. Yield: 8 servings.

♥ PATIO FOILED DINNER ♥

½ lb. hamburger
1½ c. potatoes, cubed
1 c. carrots, cubed
½ c. onion, diced

1 tsp. salt
Pepper
½ tsp. dry onion soup mix

Shape hamburger into 2 patties. Cut 2 (12-inch) pieces of foil. On each piece place 1 patty and ½ of the potatoes, carrots and onions. Season well with salt and pepper. Add ¼ teaspoon soup mix to each. Fold sides up over food and secure. Fold ends over several times so juices do not leak through. Bake in 400° oven or over grill for 1 hour. Yield: 2 servings.

♥ BEEF STEW ♥

2 lbs. stew meat, cut in 1-inch
  cubes
1 pkg. dry onion soup mix
6 carrots, cut in half lengthwise

1 c. vegetable juice
2 T. tapioca
2 T. sugar

Put meat, soup mix, carrots, juice, tapioca and sugar in a heavy, covered pot or Dutch oven and bake for 4 hours at 250°. Serve contents over mashed potatoes or rice. Yield: 6 plus servings.

"Love cometh like sunshine after rain."
--William Shakespeare

♥ BEEF & BROCCOLI ♥

¾ lb. boneless sirloin beef, cut
  cross-grain in ¼-inch strips
2 tsp. soy sauce
1¼ tsp. sugar
¼ tsp. salt
1 T. dry sherry or scotch
¼ c. beef broth or water
2 tsp. oriental sesame oil

3 T. vegetable oil
1 T. fresh ginger, minced
1 T. garlic, minced
½ tsp. dried hot red pepper flakes
1 c. broccoli florets
½ c. water
1 pkg. Japanese curly noodles

Put beef in a bowl in which soy sauce, ¼ teaspoon sugar and salt have been mixed and marinate for at least 20 minutes. In a separate bowl make a sauce of sherry or scotch, beef broth or water, remaining 1 teaspoon sugar and oriental sesame oil; set aside. Heat wok and add 2 tablespoons oil. Stir-fry beef for 1 minute in small batches and transfer to a plate to keep warm. Add remaining oil and stir-fry ginger, garlic and pepper flakes for 30 seconds. Add broccoli and stir-fry mixture 1 minute. Add water and steam for 3 to 4 minutes. Meanwhile, cook, drain and rinse noodles. Add the beef and noodles to the broccoli mixture. Mix with sauce. Heat and serve. Yield: 2 large or 4 regular servings.

♥ ROMANTIC PICNIC PIZZA ♥

1 lb. hamburger, browned
1 tsp. salt
1 tsp. garlic salt
1 tsp. oregano

1 (8-oz.) can tomato sauce
½ c. green olives, sliced and stuffed
1 c. mozzarella cheese, shredded
1 pkg. hot dog buns

Mix together hamburger, salt, garlic salt, oregano, tomato sauce, olives and mozzarella. Fill hot dog buns with mixture. Wrap buns individually in tin foil and bake at 325° for 20 minutes. Yield: 8 servings.

"If love were what the rose is,
And I were like the leaf,
Our lives would grow together
In sad or singing weather."
                --Algernon Charles Swinburne

♥ DATE NIGHT PIZZA ♥

2 pkgs. yeast
2 c. warm water
1 T. + 1 tsp. sugar
1 T. olive oil
1 T. salt
4½-5 c. flour
1 (29-oz.) can whole tomatoes in
  purée or tomato sauce
1 (10-oz.) can mushrooms

1 clove garlic, crushed
2 onions, chopped and sautéed
1 lb. ground chuck, cooked
½ lb. Italian sausage, cooked
1 bell pepper, sliced
Pinch baking soda
Italian seasonings to taste
8 oz. mozzarella cheese, shredded

Dissolve yeast in warm water and 1 tablespoon sugar. Add oil and salt. Mix in 1½ cups flour and beat for 5 minutes. Add more flour as needed to make dough. Grease bowl lightly with oil and place dough in bowl to rise. Place in a warm oven that has been turned to 200° for 1 minute and then turned off for 1 hour. After dough rises, stretch onto 2 lightly oiled cookie sheets or pizza pans. To make sauce mix tomatoes, remaining sugar, mushrooms, garlic, onions, ground chuck, sausage, pepper, baking soda and seasonings. Simmer for 2 hours or cook in a crockpot for 6 to 8 hours on low or 4 hours on high. Spread sauce on dough and bake at 450° for ½ hour. Put cheese on the last 10 minutes. Yield: 2 large crusts. For dinner, serves 8. For appetizers serves 12 to 14.

♥ LOVIN' IT PIZZA DOUGH ♥

1 c. warm water
1 pkg. active dry yeast or ¼ oz.
  compressed yeast
2½-3 c. unbleached all-purpose
  flour

2 T. olive oil
½ tsp. salt

Combine water, yeast and 1½ cups flour in large bowl; mix well. Add oil and salt. With your hands or a large wooden spoon, work ingredients together, gradually adding remaining flour, until dough holds its shape. Place dough on a lightly floured surface and knead about 5 minutes or until it is smooth and elastic. If dough becomes sticky while kneading, sprinkle more flour over it. Transfer dough into a lightly oiled 2-quart bowl. Cover with plastic wrap or a towel and let rise for 1 hour or until doubled in size. When dough has risen, place it on a lightly floured surface and divide it into two or more parts. Roll into balls and cover with towel and let rise for 15 to 20 minutes. You may now shape onto pizza pans and top as desired and cook. Yield: 2 (12-inch) pizza crusts. Serves 4 as a meal; 8 appetizer portions.

♥ PERFECT PIZZA SAUCE ♥

1 (28-oz.) can Italian-style tomato
  purée
1 lg. clove garlic, minced
1 tsp. dried oregano or marjoram
4 fresh basil leaves or 1 tsp. dried
  basil

1 bay leaf
Freshly ground black pepper to
  taste

Place all ingredients in 3-quart saucepan. Cover and bring to a boil. Uncover, lower heat and simmer, stirring occasionally, for 30 minutes. Remove bay leaf and top pizzas as desired. Tops 2 (12-inch) pizzas.

♥ MARGARITA PIZZA ♥

Cornmeal
½ recipe Partners In Love Pizza
  Dough
1½ c. Love & Pizza Sauce
1½ c. mozzarella cheese, grated

8 imported black olives
6 lg. fresh basil leaves
½ tsp. salt (opt.)
Oil to taste
Pepper to taste

Preheat oven to 500° 1 hour before cooking. When the oven is almost ready, lightly oil a pizza pan and sprinkle it with cornmeal. On a well-floured work surface, press pizza dough to form a 12-inch circle. Transfer the dough to prepared pizza pan and spread sauce over it, leaving a ½-inch rim. Sprinkle cheese over sauce and arrange olives and basil leaves over cheese. Sprinkle with salt and drizzle lightly with oil, followed by sprinkling of pepper. Bake 15 to 20 minutes or until crust is golden brown. Yield: 1 (12-inch) pizza. Serves 2.

♥ SPICIN' IT UP PIZZA SAUCE ♥

8 oz. hot Italian sausage
1 (28-oz.) can Italian-style tomato
  purée
2 tsp. chile peppers, finely chopped

2 cloves garlic, minced
1 bay leaf
1 tsp. black pepper, freshly ground

Sauté the sausage in a skillet over medium heat until browned, breaking it up with fork as it cooks. Drain and set aside. In a 3-quart saucepan combine remaining ingredients. Stir in reserved sausage. Cover and bring to a boil. Uncover, lower heat and simmer for 30 minutes, stirring occasionally. Adjust seasonings to taste and top pizzas as desired. Tops 2 (12-inch) pizzas.

Precious Pork

♥ POETIC PORK ROAST ♥

1 (4-5 lb.) pork roast
1 clove garlic, halved
Pepper to taste
1 tsp. caraway seed
2 c. hot water

3 beef bouillon cubes
3 T. cornstarch, blended with 3 T.
  water
1/2 tsp. bottled brown gravy sauce
Salt to taste

Rub roast with garlic and place in heavy roasting pan. Drop remaining garlic in pan. Sprinkle meat with pepper and caraway seed. Roast, uncovered, on bottom rack of 350° oven for 2 1/2 hours or until 170° with meat thermometer, basting several times. Remove roast, discard garlic and all but 2 tablespoons fat from roasting pan. Add water and bouillon cubes to drippings and bring to a boil. Stir in cornstarch mixture and brown gravy sauce and cook until thickened. Pour over roast when serving. Yield: 6 servings.

♥ PORK CHOPS FOR TWO ♥

2 thick pork chops
Salt and pepper to taste
2 slices onion
2 slices green pepper

3-6 T. quick-cooking rice
1 (14 1/2-oz.) can stewed tomatoes
Water as desired

Brown pork chops well on both sides. Salt and pepper to taste. Place slice of onion and green pepper on each chop and cover with rice. Spoon stewed tomatoes over chops. Bake, covered, at 350° for 1 hour. If mixture is too dry add water. Yield: 2 servings.

♥ CROCKPOT CHOPS ♥

4 pork chops, fat trimmed
1 (10 1/2-oz.) can golden mushroom
  soup, undiluted

Dried minced onion to taste

Put chops in crockpot and cover with soup. Sprinkle with onion. Cook chops on low, stirring occasionally, for 8 hours or until tender. Serve with rice or mashed potatoes. Yield: 4 servings.

♥ HONEY MUSTARD PORK ♥

2 (½-lb.) pork tenderloins
¼ tsp. salt
⅛ tsp. pepper
1 tsp. olive oil
¼ c. balsamic vinegar

1 T. honey
1 tsp. Dijon mustard
1 tsp. fresh rosemary, minced
Lemon wedges (opt.)
Fresh rosemary sprigs (opt.)

Trim fat from tenderloins. Sprinkle tenderloins with salt and pepper. To a large nonstick skillet add oil and place over medium-high heat until hot. Add tenderloins and cook 10 minutes or until pork is browned. Place tenderloins on a rack in a shallow roasting pan. Combine vinegar, honey and mustard in a small bowl. Brush over loin. Bake at 400° for 30 minutes or until meat thermometer registers 160°, basting frequently with vinegar mixture. Place on serving platter and sprinkle with minced rosemary. Garnish with lemon and rosemary sprigs if desired. Yield: 4 servings.

♥ ORANGE PORK ♥

4 pork chops, ½-inch thick
Seasoning salt to taste
¼ c. orange juice

½ tsp. dry mustard
2 tsp. brown sugar
1 tsp. orange peel, chopped

Sprinkle each side of pork chops with seasoning salt. Put on rack in roasting pan and bake in 350° oven for 20 minutes. Combine remaining ingredients and begin basting chops. Continue cooking 25 minutes, basting frequently with sauce and turning chops once. Yield: 4 servings.

♥ DINNER 'ALA CHOW MEIN ♥

1 lb. lean pork steak
1 c. celery, sliced
½ c. onion, chopped
3 T. soy sauce
2 c. beef broth or 2 beef bouillon
  cubes dissolved in 2 c. boiling
  water

3 T. cornstarch
1 (3-oz.) can sliced mushrooms,
  drained with ¼ c. liquid reserved
1 (16-oz.) can Chinese vegetables,
  drained
2 T. brown gravy sauce
3 c. chow mein noodles

Trim excess fat from meat and cut it diagonally into thin strips. Lightly grease large skillet with excess fat and brown meat on both sides. Stir in celery, onion, soy sauce and beef broth. Cover and simmer 30 minutes. Blend cornstarch and reserved mushroom liquid and gradually stir into meat mixture. Add mushrooms, Chinese vegetables and brown gravy sauce. Heat to boiling, stirring constantly. Boil and stir 1 minute. Serve over chow mein noodles. Yield: 4 generous servings.

♥ STIR-FRY PORK SURPRISE ♥

6 pork loin chops
2 T. soy sauce
1 tsp. sesame oil
1/4 tsp. pepper
1 T. + 1 tsp. cornstarch
3/4 c. + 1 T. vegetable oil

1 (10-oz.) pkg. snow pea pods, fresh
  or frozen
1/4 c. water
1 (16-oz.) can apricot halves,
  drained with 1/4 c. syrup reserved
1 c. cashews (opt.)

Trim fat from pork and cube and pound meat into thin strips. Mix together soy sauce, sesame oil, pepper and 1 tablespoon cornstarch. Add meat and let marinate 15 minutes. Heat a wok or electric fry pan to high and add 3/4 cup oil. Brown meat, cooking it in oil for 3 to 4 minutes. Remove and drain meat. Discard oil and wipe out wok. Heat 1 tablespoon oil in wok. Add snow peas and cook 30 seconds. Add water, cover and steam for 30 seconds. Add meat and apricots and cook another 30 seconds. Dissolve 1 teaspoon cornstarch in apricot syrup and add to meat. Cook until thick and clear. Serve mixture over hot rice and garnish with cashews. Yield: 6 servings.

♥ SPAGHETTI FOR LOVERS ♥

4 scallions, thinly sliced
1 clove garlic, minced
4 stalks celery, sliced
Olive oil
4 tomatoes or fresh asparagus
  spears, chopped

1 ham steak, cubed
Salt and pepper to taste
1/2 lb. spaghetti
Parmesan cheese, grated

Sauté scallions, garlic and celery in olive oil. Add tomatoes or asparagus and ham. Season with salt and pepper. Set aside and keep warm. Cook spaghetti according to package directions until al dente. Drain well and toss into the sauté mixture. Add more olive oil, if desired. Divide into servings and top with Parmesan cheese. Yield: 4 servings.

♥ TANGY HAM ♥

1/4 c. mustard
1/4 c. pineapple juice
2 T. sugar
1/2 tsp. horseradish

Dash salt
1 (1-inch thick) precooked ham
  steak

Mix mustard, pineapple juice, sugar, horseradish and salt in saucepan and heat for 10 minutes. Place ham steak on greased grill over hot coals. Baste frequently with heated sauce. Grill 5 to 7 minutes per side until steak is done. Yield: 2 servings.

♥ SWEETHEART SPARE RIBS ♥

2-3 lb. pork spare ribs
$^1/_2$ tsp. ginger
1 clove garlic
$^1/_2$ c. soy sauce

$^3/_4$ c. sugar
$^1/_2$ c. ketchup
$^3/_4$ tsp. salt

Cover ribs with water and boil for 1 hour before draining. Mix rest of ingredients in baking dish. Put ribs in dish and marinate for 2 hours. Bake contents at 350° for one hour. Yield: 3 to 4 servings.

Pleasing Poultry

♥ PICNIC FRIED CHICKEN ♥

$^1/_2$ tsp. dried thyme, crushed
$^1/_2$ tsp. dried marjoram, crushed
$^1/_2$ tsp. celery salt
1 tsp. salt
$^1/_4$ tsp. pepper

1 (2$^1/_2$ to 3-lb.) broiler-fryer
  chicken, cut up
$^1/_3$ c. flour
3 T. shortening

Combine seasonings and sprinkle over chicken pieces. Roll in flour. Slowly brown chicken pieces in melted shortening about 15 minutes, being careful not to crowd pieces. Reduce heat and cover. Cook 30 to 40 minutes or until tender. Uncover the skillet the last 10 minutes. Yield: 4 servings.

♥ CHICKEN CACCIATORE ♥

4 boneless, skinless chicken breasts,
  chunked
Salt and pepper to taste
Flour
Paprika
4 T. olive oil, divided
2 cloves garlic, minced
1 (26-oz.) jar tomato and basil
  pasta sauce

1 sm. green bell pepper, cut into
  thin strips
1 sm. red bell pepper, cut into thin
  strips
1 ($^1/_2$-lb.) pkg. thin spaghetti,
  uncooked
1 c. (4-oz.) provolone cheese,
  shredded

Season chicken with salt and pepper. Coat with flour and sprinkle with paprika. In large skillet heat 3 tablespoons oil. Brown chicken and garlic; drain. Stir in pasta sauce and bring to a boil. Reduce heat and cover. Simmer 20 minutes, adding peppers after 15 minutes. Prepare spaghetti according to package directions. Drain and toss with remaining oil. Arrange on warm serving platter and top hot chicken with sauce and cheese. Serve immediately. Yield: 4 servings.

♥ SWEETIE CHICKEN POT PIE ♥

1⅔ c. frozen mixed vegetables, thawed
1 c. chicken, cooked and diced
1 (10½-oz.) can condensed cream of chicken soup
1 c. baking mix
½ c. milk
1 egg

Heat oven to 400°. Mix vegetables, chicken and chicken soup in ungreased pie plate. Stir remaining ingredients with fork until blended. Pour into pie plate. Bake 30 minutes or until golden brown. Yield: 2 servings.

♥ MOZZARELLA CHICKEN ♥

1 lg. boneless skinless chicken breast
Garlic to taste
1 c. prepared spaghetti sauce
2 oz. mozzarella cheese
Salt and pepper to taste
Garlic bread (opt.)

Lightly brown chicken breast and garlic in skillet over medium heat about 3 minutes on each side. Place browned chicken breast in small baking dish and cover with spaghetti sauce. Bake at 350° for 30 minutes. Remove from oven and top with mozzarella cheese. Return to oven for 15 minutes or until cheese melts. Split breast in half and serve with garlic bread. Yield: 2 servings.

♥ HONEYMOONER'S CHICKEN ♥

2 tsp. salt
1 tsp. lemon juice
1 T. oil
⅓ c. honey
1 T. prepared mustard
½ tsp. oregano
1 whole chicken, cut in pieces

Mix salt, lemon juice, oil, honey, mustard and oregano together and spoon half over chicken that has been placed in a baking dish. Bake 1 hour at 350°. When chicken is almost done, put rest of honey mixture on and continue baking. Yield: 4 servings.

♥ CHICKEN-BROCCOLI BAKE ♥

1 (6-oz.) pkg. instant stuffing mix
1 (10-oz.) pkg. frozen broccoli
1 (10-oz.) can cream of chicken soup
1 soup can water
3 chicken breasts, cooked and cut in large pieces
1 c. Colby cheese, grated

Prepare stuffing according to package directions. Thaw broccoli. Mix soup with water. Layer all ingredients in order given in a 9-inch square baking dish. Cover with foil and bake for 30 minutes at 350°.

♥ TENDER ROAST CHICKEN ♥

1 (4 to 5-lb.) roasting chicken
Salt and pepper to taste
Juice of ½ lemon
¼ tsp. oregano

2 T. butter, melted
2 c. water
2 T. olive oil

Wash and clean chicken and wipe dry. Salt and pepper chicken. Rub chicken with lemon juice and sprinkle with oregano. Add rest of ingredients and roast at 375° in covered pan for about 1 hour. Yield: 4 to 6 servings.

♥ PARTY CHICKEN ♥

1 c. salad dressing
½ c. Parmesan cheese, grated

2 tsp. oregano
2-3 lbs. chicken pieces

Mix salad dressing, cheese and oregano. Spoon mixture over chicken pieces and bake 45 minutes at 375°. Yield: 4 to 6 servings.

♥ NEVER ENDING NUGGETS ♥

4 boneless, skinless chicken breasts
1 pkg. saltine crackers
2 eggs

¼ c. milk
2 T. chicken bouillon

Cut chicken into cubes and set aside. Using food processor grind crackers into fine crumbs. Mix eggs together with milk and bouillon. Dip chicken cubes into egg mixture and then into cracker crumbs to coat well. Fry in skillet until golden brown. Serve hot. Yield: 4 servings.

♥ SWEET & SOUR CHICKEN ♥

1 c. barbecue sauce
1 c. apricot preserves
1 pkg. dry onion soup mix
2 chicken breasts, skinned and cut
  into bite-size pieces
1 tsp. garlic powder

¼ tsp. cumin
½ tsp. pepper
½ tsp. salt
1 green bell pepper, sliced or diced
1 (20-oz.) can pineapple chunks,
  drained

Heat oven to 350°. Mix barbecue sauce, preserves, soup mix, chicken and spices. Pour into a 9 x 12-inch pan. Cover and bake 45 minutes. Uncover and add bell pepper and pineapple chunks. Bake 30 minutes, uncovered. Serve over steamed white rice, mashed potatoes or noodles. Yield: 2 servings.

♥ SESAME CHICKEN ♥

2 T. sesame seeds
3 T. honey
¼ c. Marsala or dry sherry
¼ c. Dijon mustard

1 T. lemon or orange zest
1 T. lemon juice
4 boneless, skinless chicken breasts

Toast sesame seeds at 325° for 5 to 10 minutes or until lightly browned. Pour into a small bowl and add honey, Marsala, mustard, zest and lemon juice. Place chicken in shallow ovenproof baking dish and pour honey mixture over top. Turn to coat evenly with sauce. Bake at 325° for 15 to 20 minutes or until thickest part of chicken is no longer pink. Baste occasionally. Yield: 4 servings.

♥ CHARMING CHICKEN KIEV ♥

2 lg. (8-oz.) boneless, skinless
  chicken breast halves
Salt and pepper to taste
2 (2 x 2½ x ½-inch) sticks Havarti
  or Provolone cheese
1 green onion, thinly sliced
1 T. pecans, walnuts or almonds,
  finely chopped

1 egg, beaten
1 T. water
2 T. all-purpose flour
3 T. pecans, walnuts or almonds,
  ground
1 T. cooking oil

Rinse chicken and pat dry. Place each breast half between two pieces of plastic wrap. Working from center to the ends, pound the chicken lightly with flat side of meat mallet until it is ⅛ inch thick. Remove plastic wrap and season chicken lightly with salt and pepper. To assemble, place one piece of cheese in center of each chicken piece. Sprinkle with half onion and half chopped nuts. Fold in sides and roll up jellyroll style, pressing the edges to seal. In a bowl stir together egg and water. Then coat each chicken roll with flour, dip into egg mixture, and roll in ground nuts. Cover and chill rolls for 30 minutes to 24 hours. In medium skillet cook the chicken rolls in hot cooking oil over medium-high heat about 5 minutes or until golden brown, turning to brown all sides. Transfer chicken to a 8 x 8-inch or 10 x 6 x 2-inch baking dish. Bake in a 400° oven for 15 to 18 minutes or until chicken is tender and no pink remains. Yield: 2 servings.

"Love is...born with the pleasure of looking at each other, it is fed with the necessity of seeing each other, it is concluded with the impossibility of separation!"

--José Martí

♥ CARING SHISH KABOB ♥

¼ c. soy sauce
¼ c. cider or red wine vinegar
2 T. honey
2 T. salad oil
1 green onion, minced

2 lg. chicken breasts, cubed
Green peppers, cut into squares
Onions, cut into squares
Mushrooms

Combine soy sauce, vinegar, honey, salad oil and onion and use to marinate chicken for several hours. Skewer chicken along with green peppers, onions and mushrooms. Grill skewers until chicken is tender and no longer pink. Yield: 4 servings.

♥ LOVELY LEMON CHICKEN ♥

⅓ c. honey
¼ c. lemon juice
2 tsp. dried rosemary leaves,
   crushed

¼ tsp. basil
4-6 boneless, skinless chicken
   breasts

Combine honey, lemon juice, rosemary leaves and basil. Brush half of sauce over chicken. Bake at 350° for 1 hour. Brush occasionally with rest of sauce. Yield: 4 to 6 servings.

♥ ITALIAN CHICKEN ♥

2 boneless, skinless chicken breasts   Italian bread crumbs
Italian salad dressing

Marinate chicken breasts in salad dressing for 10 to 15 minutes. Dredge in bread crumbs. Place on cookie sheet and bake at 350° for 30 minutes. Yield: 2 servings.

♥ CHICKEN BREASTS FOR A COUPLE ♥

1 pkg. chipped beef
4 strips bacon
4 boneless chicken breasts

1 c. sour cream
½ (10½-oz.) can mushroom soup

Grease baking dish and line dish with chipped beef. Wrap 1 bacon slice around each chicken breast and place in dish. Mix sour cream and mushroom soup and pour over chicken breasts. Bake at 275° for 3 hours. Serve over rice. Yield: 2 to 4 servings.

♥ FOREVER TURKEY CASSEROLE ♥

1 pkg. instant stuffing mix
1½-2 c. turkey, cooked and cubed
1 (8-oz.) ctn. sour cream

1 (10½-oz.) can cream of
  mushroom soup
Cheddar cheese, shredded (opt.)

Prepare stuffing according to package directions. Layer turkey in greased casserole dish. Mix sour cream and soup and pour over turkey. Top with prepared stuffing. Top with Cheddar cheese as desired. Bake in 350° oven for 30 minutes. Yield: 8 to 10 servings.

Sassy Seafood

♥ LEMON GARLIC HALIBUT ♥

3 cloves garlic, minced
2 tsp. olive oil
3 T. fresh basil, chopped
½ tsp. or less salt

1 tsp. pepper
3 T. lemon juice
2 tsp. fresh parsley, chopped
4 (5 to 6-oz.) halibut fillets

In bowl combine garlic, oil, basil, salt, pepper, lemon juice and 1 teaspoon parsley. Pour liquid over fish and marinate in refrigerator at least 2 hours. Place fish on broiler pan or grill, reserving liquid. Broil about 5 minutes on each side. Brush with marinade and heat 1 minute more. Garnish with remaining parsley and serve. Yield: 4 servings.

♥ HALIBUT WITH SALSA ♥

1 (4-oz.) can green chiles, diced
1 Anaheim chili, seeded and
  chopped
¼ c. fresh cilantro
2 cloves garlic
2 T. onion, chopped
2 slices fresh ginger

¼ c. lime juice or white wine
  vinegar
1 tsp. lime zest
¼ tsp. salt
4 halibut or tuna steaks
Olive oil

Prepare sauce by combining all ingredients but steaks and olive oil in a food processor and mixing until smooth; set aside. Brush fish lightly with oil. Broil or grill steaks 4 to 5 minutes on each side or until fish flakes easily with fork. Serve topped with sauce. Yield: 4 servings.

♥ MARINATED FISH ♥

1 lb. firm fish (swordfish, halibut, shark, mahi-mahi, tuna, marlin, etc.)
½ c. soy sauce
¼ c. dry sherry or chicken broth, defatted

2 T. olive oil
1 T. brown sugar
2 cloves garlic, minced
2 T. fresh ginger, minced
1 T. orange zest

Place fish in shallow dish. Whisk together remaining ingredients and pour over fish. Marinate 30 minutes and drain well. Broil or grill fish for 10 minutes per inch of thickness or until fish flakes easily with fork. Baste frequently with marinade while cooking. If fish is more than 1-inch thick turn it once during cooking. Yield: 2 servings.

♥ FOREVER FOILED FISH ♥

4 fresh or frozen fish fillets
½ c. buttermilk salad dressing
2 c. broccoli florets

1 bell pepper, cut into strips
1 sm. onion, thinly sliced

Place fish fillets individually on four 12-inch squares of aluminum foil. Spoon 2 tablespoons dressing over each fillet and surround with ¼ of vegetables. Seal packets. Bake at 450° for 20 to 25 minutes for fresh fish or 35 minutes for frozen. Yield: 4 servings.

♥ ROMANTIC RED SNAPPER ♥

2 lbs. red snapper fillets
Vegetable oil
½ lb. fresh mushrooms, sliced
2 T. green onion, chopped
3 T. butter
½ tsp. salt

1 tsp. dried basil
¼ tsp. pepper
1 med. tomato, chopped
1 c. Cheddar cheese, shredded
1 egg, beaten

Place fish on lightly oiled rimmed baking sheets. Sprinkle oil on each fillet. Bake at 500° for 6 to 8 minutes or until fish flakes. Remove from oven and drain off juices. While fish is cooking sauté mushrooms and onions in butter until liquid evaporates. Remove from heat. Stir in remaining ingredients. Spoon mixture evenly over top of each fillet. Broil 5 inches away from heat until cheese melts and is bubbly. Yield: 4 servings.

♥ ORANGE ROUGHY ♥

2 orange roughy fillets   **2 T. lemon juice**
2-4 T. butter   **1 tsp. dried dill weed**

Spray glass baking dish with cooking spray and arrange fish fillets in dish. Melt butter in microwave and mix with lemon juice and dill weed. Stir and pour over fillets. Bake at 350° for 20 to 30 minutes or until fish flakes easily with fork. Yield: 2 servings.

♥ CHEESY PUFFED FISH ♥

¾ lb. sole or flounder fillets   **¼ c. Cheddar cheese, shredded**
¼ c. mayonnaise   **1 egg white, beaten**

Preheat oven to 450°. Arrange fillets in buttered or sprayed baking dish. In bowl combine mayonnaise, cheese and egg white and spread over fish. Bake 10 minutes without opening oven door. Serve at once. Yield: 2 servings.

♥ TROUT ALMONDINE ♥

4 (6 to 8-oz.) trout fillets   **½ tsp. onion salt**
Flour   **¼ c. almonds, blanched and**
Salt   **slivered**
½ c. butter   **1 tsp. lemon juice**

Wash and dry fish. Dust trout lightly with flour and salt. Heat ¼ cup butter in large skillet. Sprinkle in onion salt. Cook all fish fillets at once until lightly browned. Remove and place on warm serving platter. Drain grease from skillet. Add remaining butter and almonds. Brown almonds slowly. Add lemon juice and when sauce foams, pour it over fish. Yield: 4 servings.

♥ SHRIMP SURPRISE ♥

1 T. vegetable oil   **1 T. chili sauce**
1 T. grated ginger   **1 T. apricot jam**
1 garlic clove, minced   **1 T. rice wine vinegar**
Pinch red pepper flakes   **Rice**
¾ lb. large-shelled shrimp   **Steamed vegetables**

Add oil to wok or large nonstick skillet. Add ginger, garlic, red pepper and shrimp and stir-fry, stirring quickly and constantly over high heat. Add chili sauce, jam and vinegar and toss well to mix ingredients. Serve over rice with steamed vegetables. Yield: 2 servings.

♥ SHRIMP FRIED RICE ♥

1 T. vegetable oil
½ c. small shrimp, cooked
1 zucchini, sliced
½ c. mixed vegetables
2 scallions, chopped

2½ c. rice, cooked
1 egg, beaten
2 T. soy sauce

Heat oil in wok or large nonstick skillet. Add shrimp, zucchini, vegetables, scallions, rice and egg. Stir-fry ingredients, stirring quickly and constantly over high heat until vegetables are tender-crisp and meat is just cooked. Add soy sauce and toss well to distribute seasonings. Yield: 2 servings.

♥ BAKED SHRIMP ♥

4 dozen boiled shrimp, peeled and
    deveined
1 lemon

4 oz. sharp Cheddar cheese, grated
Bread crumbs
2 T. butter

Place shrimp in 1-quart casserole dish. Squeeze juice of lemon over top and sprinkle with cheese. Sprinkle bread crumbs over top and dot with butter. Bake for 10 minutes at 375°. Yield: 4 servings.

♥ BARBECUED SHRIMP ♥

6 lbs. med. or lg. shrimp
Salt to taste
1 c. butter
½ c. olive oil
1 tsp. black pepper
1 tsp. red pepper
4 cloves garlic

1 T. Accent
¼ tsp. thyme
½ tsp. rosemary
1 tsp. paprika
1 tsp. cinnamon
2 c. white wine or saki
French bread (opt.)

Wash shrimp until water is clear, drain well and salt. In a saucepan melt butter. Add olive oil, all dry ingredients and wine. Preheat oven. Place shrimp in big, shallow pan or two 9 x 13-inch pans. Pour butter mixture over shrimp and turn oven to broil for 10 minutes. Stir and turn shrimp and broil for 10 minutes more. If shrimp are large, cook a little longer. Serve with hot French bread to dip in sauce. Yield: 6 servings.

"I feel again a spark of that ancient flame."

--Virgil

♥ IN-LAWS ARE COMING SCALLOPS ♥

1½ lbs. scallops
4 T. butter
2 T. lemon juice

¾ c. dry white wine
Parsley (opt.)
Lemon (opt.)

Sauté scallops in butter until they're opaque throughout. Add lemon juice and wine. Heat through and serve. Garnish with parsley and sliced lemon as desired. Yield: 6 servings.

♥ CREAMED TUNA WITH PEAS ♥

1 (10½-oz.) can cream of celery
  soup
½ c. milk
1 (7-oz.) can water-packed tuna,
  drained

1 c. peas, cooked and drained
1 T. pimentos, chopped (opt.)
Biscuits or buttered toast

Blend celery soup and milk. Next add flaked tuna, peas and pimento. Heat and serve over hot biscuits or buttered toast. Yield: 4 servings.

♥ DON'T BE A CRAB CAKES ♥

1 T. mayonnaise
1 egg, beaten
2 tsp. horseradish
½ lb. crab meat

⅓ c. bread crumbs
¼ c. celery, minced
¼ c. green pepper, minced
Butter

Combine mayonnaise, egg and horseradish. Add crab meat, bread crumbs, celery and green pepper. Form into patties. Melt small amount of butter in frying pan or on griddle. Fry patties on each side until cooked through and browned. Yield: 2 to 4 servings.

" 'Nothing, so it seems to me,' said the stranger, 'is more beautiful than the love that has weathered the storms of life...The love of the young for the young, that is the beginning of life. But the love of the old for the old, that is the beginning of--of things longer.' "

--Jerome K. Jerome

Our Favorite Recipes

SWEET
STUFF

Desserts

Preserving Wedded Bliss
A step-by-step guide for saving your wedding cake

As a new bride, you'll be jumping right from the frying pan and into the fire, so to speak. One of your first kitchen duties might be preserving and freezing part of your wedding cake. For those not familiar with this practice, tradition states that the top tier or layer of the wedding cake is saved and shared on the first anniversary.

To preserve a portion of confectionary history, professionals suggest you first wrap the cake in plastic wrap and several layers of aluminum foil before storing it in a self-sealing plastic bag in the freezer. When the anniversary day arrives, or the day before, remove the cake from the freezer and allow it to thaw for several hours before serving. According to some cooks, this works best if the top layer is made of fruitcake. Some other types of cake, especially those with butter in the frosting, may not keep as well and the couple may want to consider eating it on the one-month anniversary.

Most professionals believe there's nothing wrong with waiting a year to thaw your wedding cake. To keep moisture from forming on the frosting, they suggest thawing it at room temperature in a cake cover big enough to not touch the cake. Cakes without frosting can be unwrapped and placed in a preheated 300 degree oven for about 10 minutes before serving.

After you've done everything you can to preserve the cake, you may want to serve it in an enticing way at an anniversary party or after a romantic dinner with your mate. Even though the first anniversary is considered the paper anniversary, you don't have to use paper plates and napkins — but it does leave you more time to celebrate and takes less time to clean up. Either way, you've survived the first year and are well on your way to your silver and gold anniversaries.

Sweet Stuff

Cookies & Bars

♥ ALMOST HEAVEN BROWNIES ♥

1 c. butter
2½ c. sugar
4 eggs
1 c. flour

1 (12-oz.) can chocolate syrup
1 c. chopped nuts
⅓ c. evaporated milk
½ c. chocolate chips

In a bowl cream together ½ cup butter and 1 cup sugar. Add eggs and mix well. Add flour. Blend in chocolate syrup and nuts. Bake in a greased and floured 9 x 13-inch pan at 350° for 35 to 40 minutes. In a saucepan melt remaining butter and sugar and evaporated milk. Boil for 1 minute. Remove from heat and stir in chocolate chips. Continue stirring until mixture is thick. Spread on brownies, cut and serve. Yield: 1 dozen large brownies or 24 small.

♥ MOM'S BROWNIES ♥

¾ c. + 3 T. cocoa
3 c. sugar
1½ c. flour
1 c. margarine, melted
4 eggs

2 tsp. vanilla
½ c. nuts
¼ c. margarine
⅓ c. milk or cream

Mix ¾ cup cocoa, 2 cups sugar and flour together in a bowl. Add 1 cup melted margarine, eggs and vanilla and beat until smooth. Add nuts and stir. Pour into a greased and floured 10 x 15-inch pan. Bake for 20 minutes at 350°. In a saucepan mix remaining sugar and cocoa, ¼ c. margarine and milk. Boil mixture for 2 minutes. Let cool and beat. Frost brownies, cut and serve. Yield: 20 good sized brownies.

♥ OATMEAL CRISPIES ♥

½ c. butter
½ c. margarine
½ c. sugar

1 c. flour
1½ c. quick-cooking oats
Powdered sugar as desired

In a large bowl beat butter and margarine until creamy. Add sugar, flour and oats. Mix well. Chill and shape dough into 1 teaspoon balls. Place 3 inches apart on a greased baking sheet. Flatten balls with the bottom of a glass dipped in flour. Bake at 350° for 12 to 15 minutes. Cool and remove from baking sheet. Sprinkle with powdered sugar. Yield: 3 dozen.

♥ OATMEAL SCOTCHIES ♥

2 c. flour
2 tsp. baking powder
1 tsp. baking soda
1 c. butter
1½ c. brown sugar

2 eggs
1 T. water
1½ c. quick-cooking oats
2 c. butterscotch chips

In a large bowl mix all ingredients until well blended. Drop by teaspoonfuls onto greased cookie sheet and bake at 350° for 12 to 15 minutes or until light brown. Yield. 3 to 4 dozen.

♥ SWEETHEART SANDWICH COOKIES ♥

2 boxes chocolate cake mix
1½ c. shortening
4 eggs

1 (8-oz.) pkg. cream cheese
½ c. butter
Powdered sugar as desired

In a large bowl mix together cake mixes, shortening and eggs. Roll into 1-inch balls and place on a greased cookie sheet. Bake at 325° for 8 to 10 minutes. In a separate bowl mix together cream cheese, butter and desired amount of powdered sugar. Beat until smooth. Frost half the cookies and top with another cookie. Yield: 2 dozen.

"One word
Frees us of all the weight and pain of life:
That word is love."

--Sophocles

♥ MOLASSES COOKIES ♥

1½ c. flour
¾ tsp. baking soda
½ tsp. salt
½ c. shortening
¾ c. sugar

1 egg
¼ c. molasses
½ c. coconut, chopped fine
½ c. walnuts, chopped fine

In a small bowl sift together flour, baking soda and salt and set aside. In a large bowl blend together shortening, sugar, egg and molasses. Gradually blend in flour mixture. Add coconut and walnuts and mix well. Drop by teaspoonfuls onto greased baking sheet. Bake in a 375° oven for about 10 minutes. Yield: approximately 3 dozen.

♥ OUTRAGEOUS COOKIES ♥

½ c. sugar
⅓ c. brown sugar, lightly packed
½ c. butter, softened
½ c. peanut butter
½ tsp. vanilla
1 egg

1 c. flour
½ c. quick-cooking oats
1 tsp. baking soda
¼ tsp. salt
1 (6-oz.) pkg. chocolate chips

Heat oven to 350°. In a large bowl beat together sugars, butter, peanut butter, vanilla and egg until creamy and well blended. Mix in flour, oats, baking soda and salt. Stir in chips. Place on an ungreased cookie sheet and bake for 10 to 12 minutes. Cool 1 minute before removing from cookie sheet and serving. Yield: approximately 2 dozen.

♥ LEMON FINGERS L'AMOUR ♥

1 c. butter, softened
2¼ c. flour
1 c. powdered sugar

½ c. lemon juice
4 eggs
2 c. sugar

Mix butter, 2 cups flour and powdered sugar. Spread mixture in an ungreased 9 x 13-inch glass pan. Bake at 325° for 20 minutes. In a bowl combine lemon juice, eggs, sugar and remaining flour. Pour over crust and bake for 20 minutes longer. Sprinkle powdered sugar over top when removed from oven. Let cool before cutting into squares and serving. Yield: approximately 20 bars.

♥ PEANUT CHEWS ♥

1½ c. flour
⅔ c. brown sugar, packed
½ c. margarine, softened
3 tsp. vanilla
2 egg yolks
¼ tsp. baking soda
½ tsp. baking powder

½ tsp. salt
3 c. mini marshmallows
⅔ c. corn syrup
¼ c. margarine
1 (12-oz.) pkg. peanut butter chips
2 c. rice crispies
2 c. peanuts

In a large bowl combine flour, brown sugar, ½ cup softened margarine, 1 teaspoon vanilla, egg yolks, baking soda, baking powder and salt. Press mixture into an ungreased 9 x 13-inch pan. Bake at 350° for 12 to 15 minutes. Sprinkle with marshmallows and bake 1 to 2 minutes longer. In a saucepan heat corn syrup, ¼ cup margarine, 2 teaspoons vanilla and peanut butter chips, stirring until smooth. Add nuts and cereal and spoon mixture over crust. Chill before serving. Yield: 2 dozen.

♥ SUGAR'S COOKIES ♥

1 c. butter, softened
1 c. sugar
1 lg. egg

1 tsp. vanilla
2¾ c. flour
1 tsp. baking powder

In a large mixing bowl cream together butter and sugar until very light. Beat in egg and vanilla. Stir flour and baking powder into butter mixture. Divide dough into thirds and wrap in plastic wrap. Refrigerate for at least 2 hours. On a lightly floured surface, roll dough to ⅛-inch thickness. Cut into desired shapes and transfer to ungreased cookie sheet. Bake at 375° for about 12 minutes. Yield: 3 to 4 dozen.

♥ PEANUT BUTTER KISS KISS ♥

½ c. shortening
½ c. peanut butter, packed
½ c. brown sugar
½ c. sugar
1 egg
2 T. milk

1 tsp. vanilla
1⅓ c. flour
1 tsp. baking soda
½ tsp. salt
Sugar
Milk chocolate candies

Cream together shortening, peanut butter and sugars in a large bowl. Add egg, milk and vanilla and beat all until smooth. Stir in dry ingredients except chocolate candies. Roll into small balls and dip in sugar. Bake on a cookie sheet at 375° for 7 minutes. Remove from oven and immediately press chocolate candies into middle. Return to oven and bake for 3 minutes. Yield: 4 dozen.

BRIDE-06

♥ MEXICAN WEDDING CAKE COOKIES ♥

1 c. sifted flour
1/4 tsp. salt
1 c. pecans, finely chopped
1/2 c. butter

1 1/4 c. powdered sugar
1 tsp. vanilla
1 1/2 tsp. cold water

In a small bowl mix together flour, salt and pecans. In another bowl cream together butter and 1/4 cup powdered sugar until fluffy. Add vanilla and water. Add flour mixture to butter mixture and blend just enough to combine ingredients. Shape into small balls. Bake at 350° on a cookie sheet until light brown. While cookies are warm, shake lightly in a paper bag filled with 1 cup powdered sugar. Yield: 2 1/2 dozen small cookies.

♥ RICE CRISPIE BARS ♥

1 c. sugar
1 c. light corn syrup
1/4 c. butter
1 c. peanut butter

6 c. rice crispies
1 c. chocolate chips
1 c. butterscotch chips

In a large saucepan bring sugar, syrup and butter to a full boil. Remove from heat and add peanut butter. Mix well and add cereal. Spread in a 9 x 13-inch pan. Let mixture cool. In another saucepan melt together chocolate and butterscotch chips. Frost over rice crispie mixture, cut and serve. Yield: 12 to 15 bars.

♥ CLOUD 9 COOKIES ♥

1 1/2 c. butter, softened
1 c. brown sugar
1 c. sugar
2 eggs
2 tsp. vanilla

3 c. flour
2 tsp. cream of tartar
2 tsp. baking soda
Colored sugar (opt.)

Preheat oven to 350°. In a large bowl mix together softened butter with both sugars. Add eggs and vanilla and beat well. In a separate bowl sift together flour, cream of tartar and baking soda. Add to butter mixture. Blend well and drop by teaspoonful on ungreased baking sheets. Bake for 8 minutes. Decorate with colored sugar as desired. Yield: 8 dozen small cookies.

♥ BANANA BARS ♥

½ c. margarine
1½ c. sugar
2 eggs
2 T. lemon juice
¾ c. milk
¼ tsp. salt
2 c. flour

1 tsp. soda
2-3 ripe bananas, mashed
For My Sweet Frosting
1 tsp. vanilla
¼ tsp. nutmeg
Powdered sugar

In a large bowl mix margarine, sugar and eggs. Sour milk by adding lemon juice to milk and let it set. Add soured milk, salt, flour, soda and bananas to butter-sugar mixture and mix well. Pour mixture into a greased jelly roll pan and bake at 375° for 25 minutes. Make For My Sweet Frosting and add vanilla and nutmeg. Adjust with powdered sugar to achieve desired consistency. Frost over bars after they have cooled. Cut into squares and serve. Yield: 24 squares.

♥ FOR MY SWEET FROSTING ♥

¼ c. margarine or butter
1 tsp. vanilla

2 c. powdered sugar
2 T. milk

Melt butter over low heat. Then beat in sugar and vanilla. Stir in milk and beat well, adding more sugar or milk to create proper consistency.

Cherished Cakes

♥ PICNIC FOR TWO CHOCOLATE CAKE ♥

1⅓ c. butter, softened
2½ c. sugar
2 eggs
2½ c. flour
1 c. cocoa
2 tsp. baking soda

1 c. buttermilk
2 tsp. vanilla
1 c. boiling water
4½ c. powdered sugar
¼ c. milk

In a large bowl cream together 1 cup butter and regular sugar. Add eggs and mix well. In a separate bowl combine flour, ½ cup cocoa and baking soda. Add to butter mixture alternately with buttermilk and ½ teaspoon vanilla. Lastly, add boiling water. Pour into 9 x 13-inch baking pan and bake at 350° for 30 to 40 minutes. In another bowl beat remaining butter until fluffy. Gradually add 2 cups of powdered sugar, beating well. Slowly beat in milk and remaining vanilla. Slowly beat in remaining powdered sugar and additional milk, if needed, to make a frosting consistency. When cake has cooled, frost as desired. Yield: 12 generous squares.

♥ GOEY CHOCOLATE CAKE ♥

1 pkg. German chocolate cake mix
1 lg. pkg. chocolate pudding mix

1 (8-oz.) ctn. whipped topping
Crushed butter brickle or toffee
  candy

Mix cake mix as directed and bake in 9 x 13-inch pan at 350°. Let cool. Cook pudding as directed and let cool. Turn cake out on heavy cardboard sheet covered with foil. Cover top of cake with pudding and then with whipped topping. Sprinkle crushed candy over top. Refrigerate and serve chilled. Yield: 10 to 12.

♥ LUNCHBOX CUPCAKES ♥

1 pkg. chocolate cake mix
1 (8-oz.) pkg. cream cheese,
  softened
1½ tsp. vanilla

⅓ c. sugar
1 egg
Mini chips

Mix chocolate cake mix according to package directions. Spoon into lined cupcake pans. Mix cream cheese, vanilla, sugar and egg. Beat until smooth. Drop 1 teaspoon of cream cheese filling into the center of each cupcake. Sprinkle with mini chips. Bake at 350° for 25 to 30 minutes. Yield: 2 dozen.

♥ CARING CARROT CAKE ♥

1 c. all-purpose flour
¾ c. sugar
1 tsp. cinnamon
½ tsp. salt
½ tsp. baking soda
½ tsp. baking powder

¼ tsp. ground nutmeg
1½ c. carrots, grated
½ c. oil
¼ c. water
2 eggs, lightly beaten
½ tsp. vanilla

Combine flour, sugar, cinnamon, salt, baking soda, baking powder and nutmeg in a 9-inch baking pan. Add carrots, oil, water, eggs and vanilla. Stir briskly with a fork until well blended. Bake at 350° for 30 minutes. Yield: 6 to 8 servings.

"Love conquers all things; let us too surrender to Love."
--Virgil

♥ BETTER THAN SEX CAKE ♥

1 pkg. German chocolate cake mix
1 (10½-oz.) can sweetened
  condensed milk
1 (15-oz.) jar butterscotch-caramel
  ice cream topping

1 (8-oz.) ctn. whipped cream
  topping
2-3 toffee candy bars

Bake cake according to package direction in a 9 x 13-inch pan. Remove from oven and poke holes in the cake with the handle of a wooden spoon. Pour condensed milk in holes and pour ice cream topping over milk. Frost with whipped topping. Crush candy bars and sprinkle over top. Refrigerate until served. Yield: 12 servings.

♥ BUTTER POUND CAKE ♥

1 (8-oz.) pkg. cream cheese,
  softened
½ c. water, warm
2 T. butter, melted

1 pkg. yellow butter cake mix
4 eggs
½ c. sugar
½ c. oil

Mix together cream cheese, water and butter. Add cake mix, eggs, sugar and oil. Mix well approximately 3 to 4 minutes. Pour into a greased tube or a floured bundt pan. Bake at 350° for 40 to 45 minutes. Yield: 8 to 10 servings.

♥ MARMALADE CAKE ♥

1 T. butter, melted
½ c. orange marmalade or favorite
  jam
2 T. nuts, chopped

1 c. brown sugar, packed
1 tsp. cinnamon
2 (12-oz.) pkgs. biscuits
½ c. butter, melted

Grease bundt pan with 1 tablespoon melted butter. Spoon marmalade into pan. Sprinkle in nuts. Mix together brown sugar and cinnamon. Dip biscuits in ½ c. melted butter, then in sugar mixture. Stand biscuits on edge of bundt pan. Sprinkle with remaining sugar mixture. Bake at 350° for 30 to 40 minutes or until brown. Cool 5 minutes and remove from pan. Yield: 8 to 10 servings.

"But there's nothing half so sweet in life
As love's young dream."

--Thomas Moore

♥ CREAM CHEESE CUDDLE CAKE ♥

2 (3-oz.) pkgs. cream cheese
2 (12-oz.) pkgs. biscuits
½ c. sugar

1 tsp. cinnamon
3 T. butter, melted
½ c. pecans, chopped

Heat oven to 375°. Cut cream cheese into 20 pieces; shape into balls. Roll each biscuit out on pastry cloth to 3-inch diameter. Combine sugar and cinnamon. Place 1 cheese ball and 1 teaspoon cinnamon mixture on each biscuit. Fold biscuit around mixture and pinch dough to seal. Pour melted butter into bottom of greased 9-inch round cake pan. Sprinkle nuts and remaining cinnamon mixture into pan. Place rolls on top of mixture, seam side up. Bake about 25 minutes or until brown. Cool 5 minutes and invert onto serving plate. Yield: 4 servings.

Cutie Pies

♥ APPLE OF MY EYE PIE ♥

6-7 Golden Delicious apples, peeled,
  cored and sliced
2 T. lemon juice
1½ c. sugar
2 tsp. ground cinnamon
¼ tsp. ground nutmeg
¼ tsp. ground allspice

Dash salt
3 T. cornstarch
½ c. water
3 T. butter
2 unbaked pie crusts

Toss apples with lemon juice and set aside. In a saucepan combine sugar, cinnamon, nutmeg, allspice, salt and cornstarch. Add water and butter, mixing well. Bring to a boil over low heat, stirring occasionally. Remove from heat and toss with sliced apples. Turn mixture into pie crust and cover with a top crust. Seal sides and make slits in top crust. Place foil sheet on rack about 2 inches below pie as pie will be juicy and may run over. Bake at 350° for 50 to 60 minutes or until crust is golden brown. Yield: 6 servings.

"With love's light wings did I o'er-perch these walls;
For stony limits cannot love hold out,
And what love can do that dares love attempt."
                                        --William Shakespeare

♥ CRAZY PEACH PIE ♥

4 lg. peaches	3 egg yolks
1 (9-inch) unbaked pie crust	1¼ c. sugar
1 (8-oz.) ctn. sour cream	¾ c. flour
1 tsp. vanilla	4 T. butter

Preheat oven to 425°. Peel peaches, slice and arrange them in the pie shell. With wire whisk, beat sour cream, vanilla, egg yolks, 1 cup sugar and ¼ cup flour until well blended. Pour mixture over peaches in the pie shell. Place pie in oven and bake for 30 minutes. Meanwhile, mix butter and remaining flour and sugar until mixture resembles coarse crumbs. After pie is done sprinkle mixture over top. Return to oven and bake 15 minutes longer. Refrigerate until cooled. Yield: 6 servings.

♥ PIE PASTRY ♥

3 c. all-purpose flour	1 egg, beaten
1 tsp. salt	6 T. cold water
1¼ c. shortening	1 T. vinegar

Combine flour and salt in a medium bowl. Cut in shortening until mixture resembles coarse crumbs. In a separate bowl blend egg, water and vinegar with spoon. Pour into flour. Blend with spoon to form into a ball. Refrigerate until ready to roll into pie crust. Yield: 2 (10-inch) crusts or 3 (8-inch) crusts.

♥ FOOLPROOF MERINGUE ♥

3 lg. egg whites	1 c. marshmallow cream
Dash salt	

Beat egg whites and salt until soft peaks form. Gradually add marshmallow cream, beating until stiff peaks form. Spread over pie filling, sealing to edge of crust. Bake at 350° for 12 to 15 minutes or until lightly browned. Cool before serving. Yield: 1 pie top.

♥ BEST FRIEND'S PIE ♥

2 c. ice cream	1 pkg. instant chocolate pudding
1 c. milk	1 prepared graham cracker crust

Stir ice cream, milk and pudding well. Turn mixture into pie crust and freeze before serving. Yield: 6 servings.

♥ FRESH STRAWBERRY PIE ♥

3 T. cornstarch
1 c. sugar
2 T. light corn syrup
1 c. water

1 pkg. strawberry gelatin
1 qt. strawberries, sliced
1 prepared pie crust
Whipped topping

Cook cornstarch, sugar, corn syrup and water in the microwave for 4 minutes or until thick and bubbly. Add strawberry gelatin, mix and cool. Add sliced strawberries and pour mixture into pie crust. Top pie with whipped topping and garnish with extra strawberries. Yield: 6 servings.

Darling Desserts

♥ HARVEST BAKED APPLES ♥

4 lg. Cortland or Rome apples
¾ c. brown sugar
½ c. walnuts, chopped

2 T. butter
½ tsp. cinnamon
1 c. apple juice or cider

Preheat oven to 350°. Core and pare apples ⅓ of the way down to prevent skin from splitting. Set in deep baking dish. In a separate bowl combine brown sugar, walnuts, butter and cinnamon and fill apples. Pour juice around apples. Bake 25 minutes and serve warm. Yield: 4 servings.

♥ APPLE DUMPLING OF MY EYE ♥

1 (5-oz.) can buttermilk biscuits
2½ med. cooking apples, peeled,
  cored and quartered
¾ c. sugar

¾ c. water
¼ c. butter
⅓ tsp. vanilla extract

Roll each biscuit into a 5½-inch circle on a lightly floured surface. Cut each circle in half. Place one apple quarter on each piece of dough. Moisten edges of dough with water and bring ends to center, pinching to seal. Place dumplings in a baking dish. Repeat procedure with remaining dough and apples. Combine sugar, water, butter and vanilla extract in a saucepan. Cook over medium heat until mixture comes to a boil. Pour syrup over dumplings. Bake at 350° for 30 minutes or until dumplings are golden brown. Baste frequently with syrup. Yield: 4 servings.

♥ APPLE CRISP ♥

5 Granny Smith apples
¼-½ c. cinnamon and sugar mixture

½ box yellow cake mix
½ c. butter, melted

Peel, core and slice apples. Place apples in a greased 9 x 13-inch baking dish and sprinkle sugar mixture over top. Sprinkle with cake mix and drizzle with melted butter. Bake at 350° for 30 minutes. Serve warm. Yield: 8 to 12 servings.

♥ PEACH KISSES COBBLER ♥

½ c. butter
1 (15-oz.) can peaches, drained
1 c. flour

1 c. milk
1 c. sugar

Preheat oven to 350°. Melt butter and pour over peaches that have been placed in a buttered 8-inch baking dish. In a separate bowl mix flour, milk and sugar. Pour over peaches. Bake contents at 350° for about 1 hour. Yield: 6 servings.

♥ SWEET FUDGE FOR MY SWEETIE ♥

1⅓ c. sugar
¼ c. butter
¼ tsp. salt
⅔ c. evaporated milk
1 (7-oz.) jar marshmallow cream

1 (12-oz.) pkg. semi-sweet chocolate chips
1 tsp. vanilla
1 c. walnuts, coarsely chopped

In a saucepan mix sugar, butter, salt, milk and marshmallow cream. Boil mixture for 5 minutes and add chocolate chips, vanilla and walnuts. Put mixture into buttered 8-inch square pan. Cool and cut into squares before serving.

♥ PEANUT BUTTER FUDGE ♥

1½ c. butter
1 (18-oz.) jar peanut butter

1 tsp. vanilla
1½ lbs. powdered sugar

Melt butter and peanut butter together in a large bowl in the microwave. Add vanilla and mix well. Mix with enough powdered sugar to make a thick consistency. Pour into buttered 8-inch square casserole dish and cool. Cut into squares before serving. Yield: 64 (1-inch) squares.

♥ PEANUT BRITTLE FOR MY BEAU ♥

1 c. raw peanuts
1 c. sugar
½ c. corn syrup
⅛ tsp. salt

1 tsp. butter
1 tsp. vanilla
1 tsp. baking soda

In a 1½-quart casserole dish, stir together peanuts, sugar, syrup and salt. Cook in microwave for 4 minutes on high. Stir and cook 4 more minutes. Add butter and vanilla, stirring well. Cook 2 more minutes. Add baking soda and stir until light and foamy. Immediately pour into lightly greased baking sheet. Cool 15 minutes and break into pieces.

♥ CHERRY CHEESECAKE ♥

1⅔ c. graham cracker crumbs
¼ c. butter, melted
3 (8-oz.) pkgs. cream cheese
1 c. sugar

1½ tsp. vanilla
3 eggs, beaten one at a time
Cherry pie filling

Make graham cracker crust using graham cracker crumbs and butter. Press into pie plate. In a bowl cream together cream cheese, sugar, eggs and vanilla until well blended. Pour over pie crust and bake for 20 minutes in 325° oven. Cool and top with pie filling. Yield: 6 servings.

♥ LOVIN' LEMON CHEESECAKE ♥

1 (8-oz.) pkg. cream cheese,
  softened
1 (10½-oz.) can sweetened
  condensed milk

½ c. lemon juice
1 graham cracker pie crust

In a small bowl mix together cream cheese, milk and lemon juice. Pour into prepared pie crust and chill before serving. Yield: 6 servings.

"In every house of marriage there's room for an interpreter."

--Stanley Kunitz

♥ PARTY CHERRY CHEESECAKES ♥

2 (8-oz.) pkgs. cream cheese,
  softened
¾ c. sugar
1 T. lemon juice

2 eggs
1 tsp. vanilla
Vanilla wafers
1 (21-oz.) can cherry pie filling

In a large bowl beat together cream cheese, sugar, lemon juice, eggs and vanilla until light and fluffy; set aside. Line muffin tins with paper baking cups and place 1 vanilla wafer in bottom of each cup. Fill cups ⅔ full with cheese mixture. Bake in 375° oven for 15 to 20 minutes or until set. Top each cake with 1 tablespoon cherry pie filling and chill before serving. Yield: approximately 2 dozen.

♥ OLD-FASHIONED VANILLA ICE CREAM ♥

4 eggs
2½ c. sugar
4 c. cream

6 c. milk
1½ T. vanilla
½ tsp. salt

In a large bowl beat eggs well. Add sugar to beaten eggs and mix until stiff. Add remaining ingredients and mix well. Using a commercial ice cream freezer, pour into 1 gallon ice cream container, place in ice cream freezer and freeze until solid. Yield: 6 to 8 generous servings.

♥ HOT FUDGE SAUCE ♥

¾ c. semi-sweet chocolate chips
¼ c. butter

⅔ c. sugar
1 (5-oz.) can evaporated milk

In a small heavy saucepan melt chocolate chips and butter. Add sugar and gradually stir in milk. Bring contents to a boil and reduce heat. Boil gently over low heat for 8 minutes, stirring frequently. Remove from heat and serve warm over ice cream. Yield: 6 to 8 generous servings.

"Coming together is a beginning; keeping together is progress; working together is success."

--Henry Ford

♥ DOUBLE THE FUN DESSERT ♥

1 pkg. instant butterscotch pudding
1¾ c. cold milk
1 c. whipped topping
1 c. nuts, chopped and divided

1 c. prepared butterscotch ice
  cream topping
1 qt. butter pecan ice cream

Mix pudding and milk according to package instructions. Chill 15 to 20 minutes and whip until fluffy. Gently fold in whipped topping and ½ cup nuts. Refrigerate mixture 30 minutes. Drop by ⅓ cupfuls onto waxed paper-covered cookie sheet. Make a depression in center of each pile and build up sides. Freeze for several hours or overnight until firm. Remove from freezer about 15 minutes before serving. Place on individual plates. Heat butterscotch topping until warm and stir in remaining nuts. Place a scoop of ice cream in each shell and spoon warm topping over ice cream. Garnish with dollop of whipped topping and serve immediately. Yield: 8 servings.

♥ PRECIOUS PINK DESSERT ♥

40 butter crackers
¼ c. powdered sugar
¼ c. margarine, melted
1 (8-oz.) ctn. whipped topping

1 (6-oz.) can frozen pink lemonade
1 (10½-oz.) can sweetened
  condensed milk

Crush crackers and add sugar. Mix with melted margarine to make crust and press into bottom of 9 x 13-inch dish. Combine whipped topping, lemonade and condensed milk. Pour over crust. Garnish top with more crushed crackers and chill. Yield: 12 servings.

♥ CUPID'S DESSERT ♥

½ angel food cake
1 (3-oz.) pkg. instant vanilla
  pudding
1 c. milk

1 pt. vanilla ice cream
1 (3-oz.) pkg. strawberry gelatin
1½ c. boiling water
1 (10-oz.) pkg. frozen strawberries

Break angel food cake into ½-inch pieces and spread over bottom of 9 x 13-inch pan. Mix pudding with milk and beat in ice cream until somewhat softened. Pour mixture over cake pieces and place in refrigerator. Meanwhile, dissolve gelatin in boiling water. Add frozen strawberries and mix. Once mixture had begun to set, pour it over pudding and cake. Let set for at least 2 hours in refrigerator and serve chilled. Yield: 12 servings.

♥ CHOCOLATE EXTREME FOR TWO ♥

2 oz. sweet baking chocolate
2 T. egg substitute
2 tsp. sugar
¼ c. whipping cream

¼ tsp. vanilla extract
Whipped topping (opt.)
Chocolate curls (opt.)

Place chocolate in top of a double boiler and bring water to a boil. Reduce heat to low and cook until chocolate melts. In a separate bowl combine egg substitute, sugar and whipping cream and gradually stir in melted chocolate. Cook over low heat, stirring constantly, for five minutes or until thickened. Remove from heat and stir in vanilla. Spoon mixture into serving containers. Cover and chill at least 3 hours before serving. Garnish with whipped cream and chocolate curls as desired. Yield: 2 servings.

♥ CUPID'S CHERRY SNOW ♥

1 (8-oz.) pkg. cream cheese,
  softened
1 (8 oz.) ctn. whipped topping

1 graham cracker pie crust
1 (15-oz.) can cherry pie filling

Slowly blend softened cream cheese with whipped topping in a bowl. Spread over prepared pie crust and top with pie filling. Refrigerate before serving. Yield: 4 to 6 servings.

♥ ICE CREAM JELLO ♥

1 pkg. gelatin, any desired flavor
1 c. boiling water

1 c. ice cream

Dissolve gelatin in boiling water and set slightly. Add ice cream and mix well. Refrigerate until set and serve cool. Yield: 2 servings.

"Freely we serve,
Because we freely love, as in our will
To love or not; in this we stand or fall."

--John Milton

♥ CHOCOLATE ALMOND PASTRIES ♥

1¼ c. almonds, ground
¾ c. powdered sugar
¾ tsp. almond extract
1 egg white

2 oz. semi-sweet chocolate pieces,
  melted
1 (2-ct.) pkg. refrigerated pie crusts
3-4 tsp. milk

In a small bowl combine 1 cup almonds, ¼ cup powdered sugar, ½ teaspoon almond extract, egg white and melted chocolate and blend well. Heat oven to 425° and unfold pie crust and press onto floured surface. Cut crust into 24 wedges and place about ½ teaspoon almond mixture at wide end of each wedge of dough. Roll up dough, starting at wide end and rolling to opposite point. Place point side down on ungreased baking sheet and bake for 10 to 15 minutes or until light brown. Cool completely. Meanwhile, make mixture of ½ cup powdered sugar, ¼ teaspoon almond extract, milk and ¼ cup ground almonds. Combine ingredients in a small bowl until glaze consistency is reached. Drizzle glaze over pastries once they've cooled. Yield: 24 pastries.

Our Favorite Recipes

INDEX OF RECIPES

— Breakfast In Bed —

APPLE OF MY EYE ROLLS 2
APPLE SAUSAGE 5
BAKING POWDER BISCUITS 10
BREAFAST-IN-BED BAKED
  BREAKFAST 6
BREAKFAST FOR TWO 6
BREAKFAST IN BED BURRITO 7
BREAKFAST PIZZA 7
CINNAMON ROLLS FOR YOUR
  SWEETIE 2
CRUSTLESS QUICHE 8
EGG CUPS 5
"EGGS"OTIC CASSEROLE 6
FALLING IN LOVE FRENCH
  TOAST 1
FOR MY BRAN MAN MUFFINS 3
GOTCHA GRANOLA 4
HEARTY SAUSAGE GRAVY 10
ITALIAN HONEYMOON OMELET 9
KISS ME QUICHE 7
LOVE GRITS 5
MOIST COFFEE CAKE 3
OMELET OF HAPPINESS 9
PANCAKES FOR TWO 2
QUICHE OF LOVE 8
SCRAMBLED EGGS 4
SPICY SCRAMBLED EGGS 4
SWISS CHEESE OMELET 9
WONDERFUL WAFFLES 1
YOU ARE MY SUNSHINE CAKE 3

— Before Things Get Cooking —

Darling Dips & Spreads

BEER CHEESE SPREAD 14
CHILI & CHEESE DIP 12
COME BACK FOR MORE DIP 12
CUPID'S DIP 12
DRIED BEEF DIP 13
EIGHT-LAYER SPREAD 14
GUACAMOLE TO DIE FOR 11
PECAN SPREAD 14
TACO SALAD DIP 13
VEGETABLE DIP 11

Appealing Appetizers

AREN'T YOU CUTE
  ARTICHOKE SQUARES 17
CHEESY TORTILLA HUGS 15
CHICKEN WINGS 18
DON'T BE A CRAB PUFFS 20
EASY POTATO SKINS 18
GOTCHA GREEN CHILE BITES 17
MEXICAN QUICHE APPETIZER 16
NACHOS SUPREME 16
ONION-CHEESE PUFFS 19
POTATO PUFFS 19
SASSY SPINACH AND CHEESE
  SQUARES 17
SAUCY SHRIMP COCKTAIL 15
SPICY LOVE QUICHE 16
STEAMY STUFFED
  MUSHROOMS 15
ZESTY CINNAMON STICKS 18

Beverages

CHAMPAGNE MIMOSAS 22
COLD WINTER'S NIGHT COCOA
  MIX 21
CUDDLE-UP CAPPUCCINO MIX 20
EASY PEACH SHAKE 22
GOLDEN BAND PUNCH 22
GONE BANANAS & CHOCOLATE
  SHAKE 23
HOT APPLE CIDER 21
HOT TODDYS 21
MAGICAL MOCHA COOLER 23
MOCHA SNUGGLER 20
SOOTHING ALMOND TEA 22
SPICED APPLE CIDER 21
SUMMER COOLER 22

— Lovin' From The Oven —

ANGEL BISCUITS 28
BANANA BREAD 27
BEST BUDDIES CHEDDAR
  BREAD 31
BLUEBERRY MUFFINS 27
CARAMEL PECAN PASSION 26
CHEESY BEER BREAD 30
COCOA LOVE LOAF 25
CRAZY CORN BREAD 29
DANISH PUFF EASY 28

FOREVER FOCACCIA	32
HEART-SHAPED HERBED ROLLS	29
HERBED GARLIC BREAD	30
LITTLE LOVIN' BREAD STICKS	31
LOVIN' SPOONFUL ROLLS	28
PERFECT PIZZA DOUGH	32
POUND CAKE MUFFINS	26
QUICK FIX FINGER ROLLS	31
QUICK ROLLS	29
QUICK TEA RING	27
RASPBERRY MUFFINS	26
WHOLE WHEAT PIZZA DOUGH	33
WINE, CHEESE & YOU BREAD	30
YOU ARE MY HONEY BREAD	25

— Hot, Hot, Hot! —

BEEF STEW	42
BEEF VEGETABLE SOUP	36
BROCCOLI CHEESE SOUP	39
CHILI FOR LOVERS	38
COMFY CORN CHOWDER	41
CRAZY CLAM CHOWDER	42
EASY CHICKEN NOODLE SOUP	35
HEART AND HOME SOUP	37
HEARTY MAN SOUP	41
HOT AND SOUR SOUP	40
JUST LIKE MOM'S CHICKEN NOODLE SOUP	35
MINESTRONE MAMA MIA!	36
MINESTRONE SOUP	36
OOH LA LA FRENCH ONION SOUP	40
PLEASIN' POTATO SOUP	39
RED HOT TOMATO SOUP	37
SATISFYING BEAN SOUP	39
SO GREAT SANTA FE SOUP	41
SPLIT PEA SOUP	39
VEGGIE CHILI	38
WONTON LOVE SOUP	40

— Getting Fresh —

AMBROSIA FOR LOVERS	51
BROWN RICE SALAD	46
CAESAR SALAD	43
CARAMEL APPLE SWEETHEART SALAD	52
CHAMPAGNE WISHES SALAD	51
CITRUS MIXED SALAD	50
CORN AND BARLEY SALAD	46
CREAMY AND DREAMY CUCUMBERS	48
ELEGANT CRAB LOUIS	48
FRUIT COTTAGE CHEESE SALAD	51
GRANDMA'S CARROT SALAD	50
GREEN BEANS NICOISE	47
ITALIAN SALAD	45
LAYERED WITH LOVE SALAD	44
LETTUCE BE TOGETHER SALAD	43
LOVEABLE LIME GREEN SALAD	49
MACARONI SALAD	45
MARINATED BEAN SALAD	45
MELON JULEP	51
PICNIC PAIRS CHICKEN SALAD	48
POTATO SALAD L'AMOUR	47
RASPBERRY VALENTINE SALAD	49
SLAW FOR TWO	47
SPECIAL SPINACH SALAD	44
SWEET ORANGE CARROT SALAD	50
SWEETIE'S SPINACH SALAD	44
TEX-MEX CHICKEN SALAD	49
TWO PEAS IN A POD SALAD	45
WALDORF SALAD	50

— Extra Flavors, Extra Fun —

ACORN SQUASH	59
ALMOND GREEN BEANS	53
BROCCOLI CASSEROLE	62
BROCCOLI POTATO TOPPER	54
BRUSSELS SPROUTS	62
BUBBLING OVER BAKED BEANS	53
CANDIED YAMS	60
CUDDLE UP CLAM LINGUINI	68
CUDDLY CORN CASSEROLE	61
EGGPLANT PARMIGIANA	59
FAMILY FAVORTE GREEN BEAN CASSEROLE	53
FETTUCCINE FOR A COUPLE	64
FOILED GRILLED POTATOES	54
FRIED ONION RINGS	58
GLAZED CARROTS	58
HOMEMADE HASH BROWNS	57
HOT & SPICY CHILI-CHEESE RICE	65
HOT STUFF JALAPEÑO CORN CASSEROLE	61
IN PERFECT HARMONY QUICHE	66
LOVE YA BABY CARROTS	58
LOVEABLE LINGUINI	66
LOVIN' OVEN FRIES	55
MASHED POTATO CAKES	55
MASHED POTATOES	56
MELT YOUR HEART MACARONI	61
PASTA BELLA STIR-FRY	67
PEAS AND POTATOES	56
PEAS IN A POD & CARROTS	57
PERFECT PAIR PAN GRAVY	56

RIGATONI FOR TWO	65		SIMPLE GOULASH	74
SIDE BY SIDE SAVORY PEAS	57		SPICIN' IT UP PIZZA SAUCE	78
SKILLET SPUDS	54		STUFFED PEPPERS FOR TWO	74
SO SAUCY SPAGHETTI SAUCE	67		SWEETHEART SLOPPY JOES	74
SPANISH RICE	64		SWISS STEAK	71
SPICY NACHO POTATO TOPPER	54			
SPICY ORANGE BROCCOLI	63			
STEAMED OVEN RICE PILAF	63			
STEAMIN' STUFFED POTATOES	55			
STIR FRY VEGGIES	59			
STIR-FRIED BROCCOLI	63			
STUFFED ZUCCHINI FOR TWO	60			
SWEET STUFF RED CABBAGE	62			

Precious Pork

TEMPTING FETTUCCINE		
ALFREDO	66	
TOMATO-ZUCCHINI PIE	60	
VALENTINE RED BEANS AND		
RICE	65	
VEGGIE RAGOUT	64	
YOU'RE THE BEST PRIMA		
PASTA	67	

CROCKPOT CHOPS	79
DINNER 'ALA CHOW MEIN	80
HONEY MUSTARD PORK	80
ORANGE PORK	80
POETIC PORK ROAST	79
PORK CHOPS FOR TWO	79
SPAGHETTI FOR LOVERS	81
STIR-FRY PORK SURPRISE	81
SWEETHEART SPARE RIBS	82
TANGY HAM	81

— Main Squeeze —

Beloved Beef

Pleasing Poultry

CARING SHISH KABOB	86
CHARMING CHICKEN KIEV	85
CHICKEN BREASTS FOR A	
COUPLE	86
CHICKEN CACCIATORE	82
CHICKEN-BROCCOLI BAKE	83
FOREVER TURKEY CASSEROLE	87
HONEYMOONER'S CHICKEN	83
ITALIAN CHICKEN	86
LOVELY LEMON CHICKEN	86
MOZZARELLA CHICKEN	83
NEVER ENDING NUGGETS	84
PARTY CHICKEN	84
PICNIC FRIED CHICKEN	82
SESAME CHICKEN	85
SWEET & SOUR CHICKEN	84
SWEETIE CHICKEN POT PIE	83
TENDER ROAST CHICKEN	84

BEEF & BROCCOLI	76
BEEF KABOBS	71
BEEF STEW	75
BEEF STROGANOFF	70
CASSEROLE SURPRISE	72
COMPANY'S COMING PRIME	
RIB	72
CRISP HASH FOR MY HONEY	74
CROCKPOT CUBED STEAK	73
DATE NIGHT PIZZA	77
EASY & ENDEARING	
CASSEROLE	73
EXTRAVAGANT BEEF BRISKET	70
FLAVORFUL FAJITAS	71
HAMBURGER CASSEROLE	72
LOVE ON THE ROLL	73
LOVIN' IT PIZZA DOUGH	77
LOVIN' YOU LASAGNE	75
MARGARITA PIZZA	78
MARINATED STEAKS, MY	
DARLING	70
MEAT LOAF DIVINE	69
MOIST BEEF ROAST	69
PATIO FOILED DINNER	75
PEPPER STEAK FOR A NIGHT	
ALONE	73
PERFECT PIZZA SAUCE	78
PERFECT POT ROAST	69
ROMANTIC PICNIC PIZZA	76

Sassy Seafood

BAKED SHRIMP	90
BARBECUED SHRIMP	90
CHEESY PUFFED FISH	89
CREAMED TUNA WITH PEAS	91
DON'T BE A CRAB CAKES	91
FOREVER FOILED FISH	88
HALIBUT WITH SALSA	87
IN-LAWS ARE COMING	
SCALLOPS	91
LEMON GARLIC HALIBUT	87
MARINATED FISH	88

ORANGE ROUGHY   89
ROMANTIC RED SNAPPER   88
SHRIMP FRIED RICE   90
SHRIMP SURPRISE   89
TROUT ALMONDINE   89

— Sweet Stuff —

Cookies & Bars

ALMOST HEAVEN BROWNIES   93
BANANA BARS   98
CLOUD 9 COOKIES   97
FOR MY SWEET FROSTING   98
LEMON FINGERS L'AMOUR   95
MEXICAN WEDDING CAKE
   COOKIES   97
MOLASSES COOKIES   95
MOM'S BROWNIES   93
OATMEAL CRISPIES   94
OATMEAL SCOTCHIES   94
OUTRAGEOUS COOKIES   95
PEANUT BUTTER KISS KISS   96
PEANUT CHEWS   96
RICE CRISPIE BARS   97
SUGAR'S COOKIES   96
SWEETHEART SANDWICH
   COOKIES   94

Cherished Cakes

BETTER THAN SEX CAKE   100
BUTTER POUND CAKE   100
CARING CARROT CAKE   99
CREAM CHEESE CUDDLE CAKE   101
GOEY CHOCOLATE CAKE   99
LUNCHBOX CUPCAKES   99
MARMALADE CAKE   100
PICNIC FOR TWO CHOCOLATE
   CAKE   98

Cutie Pies

APPLE OF MY EYE PIE   101
BEST FRIEND'S PIE   102
CRAZY PEACH PIE   102
FOOLPROOF MERINGUE   102
FRESH STRAWBERRY PIE   103
PIE PASTRY   102

Darling Desserts

APPLE CRISP   104
APPLE DUMPLING OF MY EYE   103
CHERRY CHEESECAKE   105
CHOCOLATE ALMOND
   PASTRIES   109
CHOCOLATE EXTREME FOR
   TWO   108
CUPID'S CHERRY SNOW   108
CUPID'S DESSERT   107
DOUBLE THE FUN DESSERT   107
HARVEST BAKED APPLES   103
HOT FUDGE SAUCE   106
ICE CREAM JELLO   108
LOVIN' LEMON CHEESECAKE   105
OLD-FASHIONED VANILLA ICE
   CREAM   106
PARTY CHERRY CHEESECAKES   106
PEACH KISSES COBBLER   104
PEANUT BRITTLE FOR MY
   BEAU   105
PEANUT BUTTER FUDGE   104
PRECIOUS PINK DESSERT   107
SWEET FUDGE FOR MY
   SWEETIE   104

Publish your own Cookbook

Churches, schools, organizations, and families can preserve their favorite recipes by publishing a custom cookbook. Cookbooks make a great **fundraiser** because they are easy to sell and highly profitable. Our low prices also make cookbooks a perfect affordable **keepsake**. We offer:

- Low prices, high quality, and prompt service.
- Many options and styles to suit your needs.
- 90 days to pay and a written No-Risk Guarantee.

Order our FREE Cookbook Kit for full details:

- Call us at **800-445-6621, ext. CB**.
- Visit our web site at **www.morriscookbooks.com**.
- Mail the **postage-paid reply card** below.

✂

Discover the right ingredients for a really great cookbook!

Order our **FREE** Cookbook Kit. Please print neatly.

Name _____

Organization _____

Address _____

City _____ State _____ Zip _____

E-mail _____

Phone (_____) _____

Back Card 8-09

P. O. Box 2110
Kearney, NE 68848

Whether your goal is to raise funds or simply create a cherished keepsake, Morris Press Cookbooks has all the right ingredients to make a great custom cookbook. Raise $500–$50,000 while preserving favorite recipes.

Three ways to order our **FREE** Cookbook Kit:

- Call us at **800-445-6621, ext. CB**.
- Visit our web site at **www.morriscookbooks.com**.
- Complete and mail the **postage-paid reply card** below.